C000070690

Liverpool
in the 1980s

Liverpool

in the 1980s

Phil Thompson

First published 2006

STADIA is an imprint of
Tempus Publishing Limited
The Mill, Brimscombe Port,
Stroud, Gloucestershire, GL5 2QG
www.tempus-publishing.com

© Phil Thompson, 2006

The right of Phil Thompson to be identified as the Author
of this work has been asserted in accordance with the
Copyrights, Designs and Patents Act 1988.

All rights reserved. No part of this book may be reprinted
or reproduced or utilised in any form or by any electronic,
mechanical or other means, now known or hereafter invented,
including photocopying and recording, or in any information
storage or retrieval system, without the permission in writing
from the Publishers.

British Library Cataloguing in Publication Data.
A catalogue record for this book is available from the British Library.

ISBN 0 7524 4020 9

Typesetting and origination by Tempus Publishing Limited.
Printed in Great Britain.

Contents

Bob Paisley and Joe Fagan pictured here in the Liverpool dugout during a 1980 First Division encounter. When Paisley retired in 1983 Fagan took over as Liverpool manager and had a sensational first season, winning three major trophies.

Introduction

With Liverpool legends Bob Paisley, Joe Fagan and Kenny Dalglish in the managerial chair at Anfield, Liverpool ruled supreme in the 1980s. Fourteen major domestic and European trophies found their way into the Anfield trophy cabinet.

When the great Bob Paisley retired in 1983, it was thought that he would be an impossible act to follow. His successor at Anfield, Joe Fagan, thought differently and captured three of football's top prizes in his first year as manager. The tragic events at Heysel Stadium in 1985 hastened the departure of Fagan from the manager's job at Anfield.

Kenny Dalglish took over at the club and was an instant success. He led Liverpool to the League and FA Cup double in his very first season in charge. 'King Kenny' would go on to win both of the trophies again before his tenure as Liverpool manager drew to a close.

This book tells the story of the greatest trophy-winning decade in Liverpool Football Club's history, when world-class players of the calibre of Graeme Souness, Kenny Dalglish, Alan Hansen, Ian Rush, John Barnes and Peter Beardsley graced the Anfield turf.

Liverpool are now, once again, regarded as a force in European football after their fabulous Champions' League triumph in 2005. It is unlikely, however, that the Anfield faithful will ever witness such a golden decade as the 1980s ever again.

Chapter 1

Liverpool, under the direction of their legendary manager, Bob Paisley, entered the 1980s as the reigning League Champions. Former Anfield heroes such as Emlyn Hughes, Steve Heighway, Tommy Smith and Ian Callaghan might have departed the scene, but still the silverware kept on finding its way into the Anfield trophy cabinet.

Bob Paisley had also signed a young skinny Welsh kid from Chester in April 1980 for a £300,000 fee that would turn out to be one of the greatest pieces of transfer business that the Liverpool manager would ever conduct on behalf of the club. Ian Rush would eventually develop into the greatest goalscoring machine that had ever graced the Anfield turf.

Ian Rush took a little time to settle at Liverpool and some of the established Anfield regulars did have concerns that the kid from Flintshire would not make the breakthrough into Paisley's team. Liverpool central defender, Alan Hansen recalled:

> I remember playing for Liverpool Reserves against Preston and on the opposite side was John Blackley, who I knew from his time with Hibernian and Newcastle. Blackley asked me afterwards what I thought of Ian Rush because he hadn't been impressed. I said I believed Liverpool would sell him soon. Four years later, during which time Rush had scored about 250 goals, I was having another drink with Blackley. He recalled our earlier conversation and joked 'We're good judges, aren't we?'

Ian Rush only made a handful of appearances for Liverpool during his first full season at Anfield, the 1980/81 campaign, but he did play a part in the Reds' League Cup final triumph over West Ham in the replay at Villa Park. When it came to Liverpool's 1981 European Cup triumph, however, against Real Madrid, Rush could only sit back and take in the experience. Before too

The Liverpool fans display a banner that pays homage to Kenny Dalglish. Dalglish was a hero at Anfield from the moment he joined the club in 1977.

long the Welsh goalscoring sensation was destined to become an integral part of the Anfield trophy-winning machine.

Liverpool, somewhat surprisingly, had a disappointing season in the First Division as they entered a new decade. They finished fifth in the table, their worst showing since the 1970/71 campaign. Aston Villa took Liverpool's crown with Bob Paisley's side nine points behind them back in fifth spot. In the European Cup, however, it was a totally different story. Wins against Oulu Palloseura, Aberdeen, CSKA Sofia and Bayern Munich took them to Paris to play Real Madrid in the 1981 final. Bob Paisley was proving himself to be a superb tactician.

One of the most impressive victories in the Reds' European Cup run was the 5-0 on aggregate over two legs success against the champions of Scotland, Aberdeen. Aberdeen were an impressive outfit at this time in their history with Alex McLeish, Willie Miller, Gordon Strachan and Jim Leighton all seasoned Scottish internationals. A tough test for the Reds looked on the cards. Liverpool travelled up to Aberdeen for the first leg hoping to hold the Dons to a draw or perhaps a single goal deficit to take back to Anfield. They knew that Aberdeen manager, Alex Ferguson, would have his team chomping at the bit to show the English champions that they could match them in every way.

The three Scots in the Liverpool line-up, Souness, Hansen and Dalglish, were desperate to avoid defeat because of the ribbing that they would then have at the Scotland international get-together. Kenny Dalglish recalled:

Graeme, Alan and myself kept telling each other that if we didn't get a result we were going to get slaughtered every time we went back to Scotland. In fact, the

Alan Hansen tackles Nottingham Forest's Trevor Francis in a January 1980 FA Cup fourth round tie. Liverpool won the game 2-0, Dalglish and McDermott scoring the goals.

three of us got a lot of verbal abuse during the game, as expected. Alex Ferguson had prepared Aberdeen with typical thoroughness.

Liverpool, through an early goal from Terry McDermott, came away from Pittodrie with a fine 1-0 victory. McDermott's goal was outstanding with Ray Kennedy, Kenny Dalglish and David Johnson all exchanging passes before McDermott finished off the move with a clever chip that gave Jim Leighton no chance.

The game was marred by a bad injury sustained by Aberdeen's John McMaster after a heavy challenge from Ray Kennedy. Recalling Kennedy's tackle on his Aberdeen teammate Gordon Strachan said:

> John was starting out on one of his beautifully smooth runs, beating one man then another, then in came Ray Kennedy who felled him with a knee-high tackle which put him out of the game for a year. I'm not saying Kennedy went out to crock him, but if you use that kind of tackle, there is a fair chance that you will do your opponent some nasty harm. Ray Kennedy didn't even get a booking.

Liverpool saw off Aberdeen in the second leg at Anfield on Bonfire Night 1980 by a 5-0 scoreline. A Miller own goal and others from Neal, Dalglish and Hansen gave the Reds a comfortable passage through to the next round.

Liverpool's toughest test on their way to the 1981 European Cup final came in the semi-finals against German champions Bayern Munich. The Germans held Liverpool to a goalless draw in the first leg at Anfield and Paisley's team looked up against it to progress to the final. Bayern Munich fancied their chances in the return leg and when Kenny Dalglish had to go off injured after just seven minutes play, a place in the Paris final of the competition a month later looked distinctly remote. Bob Paisley then pulled a masterstroke. He sent on Howard Gayle for Dalglish and the young Liverpool-born winger ran the German side into the ground. Gayle tormented the Bayern defenders with his darting runs at them and they became totally unsettled. Recalling the game, Kenny Dalglish said, 'Howard Gayle came on for me and was absolutely magnificent. The Germans hadn't prepared for Howard. They knew nothing about this man who was running them ragged.'

Eventually, Gayle was replaced by Jimmy Case towards the end of the game, but Paisley's masterstroke had paid off. Bayern had been taken unawares by the introduction of Gayle and had had to resort to a series of fouls against the Liverpool winger in order to stop him.

Kenny Dalglish in action against Ipswich Town's Russell Osman in October 1980. Liverpool drew this encounter 1-1, Terry McDermott scoring for the Reds.

The Reds scored the vital away goal near the end of the game through Ray Kennedy that took them to the European Cup final. Bayern equalised through Rummenigge two minutes from the end, but the away goals rule meant that Paisley's side were through to a showdown in Paris with Real Madrid.

Bob Paisley's knack of making the right changes to the team to achieve the required result always seemed to be spot on. 'His knack of making the right decisions, such as which substitute to bring on, made Bob a great manager', Kenny Dalglish once declared. 'Bob was very decisive', he went on, 'He found it difficult to explain why he had done something, but he didn't need to, his actions spoke for themselves.'

Ian Rush was on the periphery of Liverpool's march towards the 1981 European Cup final, having not yet established a place for himself in the Reds'

Graeme Souness celebrates with Kenny Dalglish and Alan Hansen after scoring against CSKA Sofia in the European Cup quarter-final tie at Anfield in March 1981. Liverpool won the game 5-1, Souness scoring a hat-trick.

line-up. The young striker was, however, taking everything in and he spotted early on in his Anfield career that Bob Paisley was a special manager. Rush once said:

> He was never the kind of man you could sit down with and have a social conversation, but when Bob talked you listened. He was little short of being a genius when it came to football – and to human nature. He was a quiet, almost shy man, but you took in every word he said.

Liverpool went on to win the 1981 European Cup final against Real Madrid through an Alan Kennedy goal, scored during the last ten minutes of a dull final. The Spanish giants were no longer capable of playing the brilliant brand of football that had thrilled football followers throughout Europe in the late 1950s. The great names of their glorious past such as Puskas, Di Stefano and Gento were now a fading memory. The Real Madrid side of 1981 were a hard-working, hard-tackling outfit, with only Laurie Cunningham, a big money signing from West Brom, capable of the odd moment of magic. Bob Paisley's team matched Madrid when it came to fierce tackles being dished out and the Reds were delighted to have won their third European Cup, whether it was a dull final or not.

Liverpool's fabulous Scottish trio of Souness, Dalglish and Hansen celebrate their team's 1-0 victory over Real Madrid in the 1981 European Cup final in Paris. Alan Kennedy scored the Reds' winner.

Ian Rush is tackled by West Ham's Billy Bonds in Liverpool's 1981 League Cup final replay at Villa Park. Kenny Dalglish and Alan Hansen scored in Liverpool's 2-1 victory.

Kenny Dalglish scores Liverpool's opener against West Ham in the 1981 League Cup replay. West Ham's Billy Bonds and Geoff Pike are also in the picture.

Ian Rush had tasted just what it was like to be a part of a trophy-winning team at Anfield when he was selected to take Steve Heighway's place in the 1981 Football League Cup final replay. The first game at Wembley against West Ham had ended at 1-1, Alan Kennedy netting the Reds' goal. Bob Paisley decided to select Rush for the Villa Park replay and the youngster had a good game in Liverpool's 2-1 victory. Kenny Dalglish and Alan Hansen scored the goals that gave the Reds their first League Cup success in the club's history.

Bob Paisley prepared for an assault on the 1981/82 League Championship by paying out £900,000 for the outstanding Brighton central defender, Mark Lawrenson. Lawrenson was wanted by most top English teams, including Manchester United and Arsenal and Paisley had to break the Liverpool transfer record to capture him. The sight that greeted Lawrenson when he met the Reds' boss at a Liverpool hotel to complete the transfer surprised him a little, 'Bob was more like my granddad!' declared Liverpool's new signing:

> He picked me up at the hotel and there he was in slippers and a cardigan. I just thought this is like talking to my granddad. Bob was an amazing man though. On the way back to Anfield I suddenly realized that he never finished a sentence

off. He said 'you can play in plenty of positions can't you?' I told him I could and he said 'that's what you might have to do until you get into the team on a regular basis.' That's the way he was. He said very little to you. With hindsight you soon realised that if Bob didn't speak to you about football matters then he was obviously happy with you. Generally you never had long conversations with Bob Paisley.

Mark Lawrenson soon found himself a regular in Paisley's team as they mounted a remarkable challenge for the 1981/82 League title. As the New Year approached, Liverpool looked like they would slump to their lowest League position since achieving their status back in the First Division in 1962. They won only 6 of their first 17 League games and at the start of 1982 had dropped into the lower half of the table.

The turning point for Liverpool was two poor performances towards the end of December 1981 when Paisley's side were beaten by Brazilian team Flamengo 3-0 in the World Club Championship played in Tokyo and a 3-1 defeat at Anfield at the hands of Manchester City on Boxing Day. After the Flamengo game Bob Paisley remarked, 'It was just one of those games when our display was too bad to be true. We don't want any more displays like that and I'm hoping we've now got the worst out of our system.' Liverpool hadn't got 'the worst' out of their systems and were comprehensively beaten 3-1 by Manchester City at Anfield in their next game.

Apart from the result against City, matters could have been a whole lot worse for Liverpool Football Club when the Manchester City goalkeeper, Joe Corrigan, was hit by a bottle thrown from the Kop end towards the end of the game. Corrigan was knocked to the ground after being hit on the back of the head by the flying missile. Taking up the story, Corrigan, who went on to become a coach at Anfield, said, 'I remember after it happened, the Kop started to chant my name and pointed to the person who did it in the crowd. The police asked me if I wanted to prosecute. I said no, because Liverpool are one of the great clubs and I didn't want anything detrimental going against them.' Corrigan's incredible response saved Liverpool Football Club an unbelievable amount of trouble from the football authorities as well as the police and it is doubtful that it would ever be replicated in the modern-day game.

After a disastrous first half of the 1981/82 season, Liverpool went on an incredible run in the New Year. Early exits from the European Cup at the hands of CSKA Sofia and the FA Cup at Stamford Bridge against Chelsea left them free to concentrate on catching up with the likes of Ipswich and Manchester United at the top of the table. The new faces in the side such as Bruce Grobbelaar, Mark

Ian Rush celebrates scoring against Manchester City in April 1982. Liverpool won the game 5-0 at Maine Road.

Lawrenson and Ian Rush were now beginning to settle. By the start of March, Paisley's team found themselves in sixth position and also in the final of the Football League (Milk) Cup. The only blip during a sensational run in to their League campaign came against Brighton at Anfield, losing the game 1-0. After the Brighton defeat Liverpool went on a run of 11 straight victories, including a 5-1 victory at Stoke and a 5-0 success at Manchester City. Paisley's side won the title by four points from Ipswich with Manchester United nine points behind the Reds in third spot.

In his first full season in the first team at Anfield, Ian Rush scored 17 goals in 32 League appearances. Liverpool, with the League title in the bag, for once decided to drop their normally highly professional approach in pre-match preparation for the last game of the season away to Middlesbrough. Ian Rush said in his autobiography that the Liverpool side took to the field against Middlesbrough after downing quite a few beers before the match in a pub near the ground. Rush recalled:

> For once that ultra-professionalism that is drummed into you at Anfield went out of the window. This was the last day we would all be together before the end of

The Liverpool team celebrate another League title success after clinching the championship with a 3-1 victory over Spurs in May 1982.

the season and we decided to enjoy it. I'd never had a drink so close to a game before. A glass of lager was shoved in front of me. It was the first of quite a few pints in the next couple of hours.

Liverpool took to the field against Middlesbrough in a merry frame of mind, but still managed to come away with a 0-0 draw. Tottenham finished a highly creditable fourth in the race for the 1981/82 League title and former Spurs striker Clive Allen once claimed that trying to keep up with the Liverpool trophy-winning machine in the 1980s was virtually impossible. Allen said:

Anfield during that decade was truly a fortress. Liverpool could make very good sides look ordinary. Kenny Dalglish would orchestrate everything. Mark Lawrenson, Ronnie Whelan and Alan Hansen were majestic and Ian Rush was a goal machine. Then you had Ray Kennedy who'd always chip in with a goal too.

Liverpool's second trophy of a memorable 1981/82 campaign came in the League Cup against the side that Clive Allen would join from QPR a few years later. Spurs, who could boast world-class stars such as Ray Clemence, Glen Hoddle and Ossie Ardiles in their line-up, looked like they might loosen Liverpool's grip on the trophy that they would win in three consecutive seasons in the early 1980s. The Londoners had never tasted defeat in six Wembley finals and a Steve Archibald goal gave them the advantage until Ronnie Whelan popped up with a Liverpool equaliser three minutes from time. Goals from Ian Rush and Whelan, with his second goal of the game, brought the trophy back to Anfield for the second consecutive season. Rush was now beginning to display the type of goalscoring ability that had prompted Bob Paisley to pay out £300,000 for the Welsh teenager. Speaking about Rush's knack of scoring goals, Paisley once remarked, 'without even a glance, he seems to detect when a goalkeeper is off balance or out of position and therefore vulnerable to an immediate early strike. You can't teach players that.'

Although quick to praise individuals at Anfield, the Liverpool manager always maintained that their incredible success was ultimately down to a fantastic team spirit within the club. Bob Paisley said:

> We have been among the very best for nearly twenty consecutive years now. Teamwork is the key to that success. When I was a professional footballer it was barely a team game. It was essentially about individuals. At Liverpool we look for born winners and then we show them how to win as a team.

Speaking about Liverpool's second consecutive League Cup success, Kenny Dalglish once proclaimed, 'The League Cup suddenly became like the buses, you wait ages for one to arrive and then they come along in a rush.'

A sad note for Liverpool and football as a whole during the 1981/82 campaign was the sad death of the man who changed everything at Anfield when he arrived at the club in 1959. Bill Shankly's untimely death from a heart attack on 28 September 1981 shocked Merseyside to the core. He had a brilliant successor in Bob Paisley when he retired from the manager's job in 1974, but Shankly was the catalyst for most of the incredible success that Liverpool enjoyed in future decades.

PHIL THOMPSON

Born in the Kensington district of Liverpool, Phil Thompson really came to the notice of the nation with an outstanding performance in the Reds' 3-0 victory over Newcastle in the 1974 FA Cup final.

Phil Thompson, the first local lad to skipper Liverpool to European Cup glory after his team beat Real Madrid 1-0 in the 1981 Paris final.

Thompson joined Liverpool as an apprentice in 1971. He first impressed as a youngster playing in midfield for his school team and Kirkby Schoolboys. The Anfield coaching staff converted him into a defender and his superb central defensive partnership with Emlyn Hughes in the mid-1970s was a key factor in many of Liverpool's trophy-winning campaigns of that decade.

In season 1973/74, Phil Thompson cemented his place in the Liverpool first team. He did, however, play enough games in the previous campaign to win a championship winners' medal at the end of the 1972/73 campaign. International recognition was soon to follow and after impressing in the England Under-23s, Phil Thompson won 42 full international caps between 1976 and 1982.

One of his proudest moments in a glittering Anfield career was being asked to take over from Emlyn Hughes as club captain during the 1978/79 season. At this stage in his Liverpool career, Phil Thompson was now partnered at the heart of the Reds' defence by Alan Hansen. The two of them gelled perfectly and with Ray Clemence behind them, few attacks got the better of the Liverpool defence during this era in the club's history. Thompson also went on to skipper England on a number of occasions in the early 1980s.

The highlights of Phil Thompson's Liverpool career were the European Cup wins of 1978 and 1981. Thompson would have probably also featured in the 1977 European Cup-winning side, but for injury ending his involvement in the 1976/77 season at a crucial stage in the campaign.

Thompson lost the Liverpool captaincy to Graeme Souness during the 1981/82 season. Further success for Liverpool with League title wins in 1981/82 and 1982/83 added to his already impressive trophy haul at Anfield. In 1982 Thompson also picked up his second League Cup winners' medal.

When he left for Sheffield United in 1983, Phil Thompson's place in the annals of a glorious era in Liverpool Football Club's history was already assured.

KENNY DALGLISH

Anfield legend Emlyn Hughes described Kenny Dalglish as the greatest Liverpool player that he ever saw. Born in Dalmarnock, Glasgow, Dalglish originally played mainly in a midfield role for Celtic while learning his trade at Parkhead. Eventually Celtic boss, Jock Stein, selected him in a more attacking role and he went on to score 112 goals in 204 League appearances for Celtic.

Kenny Dalglish, arguably the greatest Liverpool player of all time.

Kenny Dalglish was already a superstar in Scotland when Bob Paisley decided to pay a record fee between British clubs to secure his services for Liverpool in 1977. £440,000 was the amount that Paisley paid for Dalglish; the question however was whether the supremely talented Scot could perform as well in the English League?

At the end of the 1977/78 season, during which Liverpool won another European Cup with Dalglish scoring the winner in the Wembley final against Bruges, any doubts about the Reds' capture from Celtic had been totally put to bed. Kenny Dalglish scored 30 goals in 59 games, virtually the same ratio of goals to games that he had achieved at Parkhead.

It was Dalglish's all–round play however that really impressed the Liverpool faithful. His football skill was at times of a breathtaking quality and he set up many a chance for his teammates with his deft touches and inch–perfect passes. Everyone at Anfield knew that they had found someone special to take the place of Kevin Keegan and Dalglish in many ways surpassed the performances of Keegan in the red shirt of Liverpool.

Kenny Dalglish won Europe's top club prize in just his first season at the club and in 1981 and 1984 he won two more European Cups to add to his 1978 medal. In his career at Celtic and Liverpool he won 102 international caps and in his playing career a staggering 39 medals.

The 1980s were undoubtedly Dalglish's golden period at Anfield both as a player and later as manager of Liverpool. Dalglish stepped into the manager's position at Liverpool following the Heysel Stadium tragedy in 1985 which led to Joe Fagan relinquishing his role at the helm of Anfield.

After thirteen glorious years at Anfield, Kenny Dalglish resigned as manager in February 1991. He returned to football in 1992 and led Blackburn Rovers to success in the 1994/95 Premiership campaign with their first championship in eighty-one years in the Football League. Kenny Dalglish is still revered at Anfield as one of Liverpool's true greats.

ALAN HANSEN

Born in Sauchie, Clackmannanshire, Alan Hansen was signed by Bob Paisley from Partick Thistle in 1977. The fee was £100,000 and it was one of the best pieces of transfer business that the Liverpool boss ever conducted.

Hansen took a little time to settle in on Merseyside, but when he found his feet, the Anfield faithful could see that Liverpool had a special talent on their hands. Hansen was a composed, elegant defender who made the art of keeping the opposition's attack at bay look relatively easy. Eventually he formed impressive partnerships, first with Phil Thompson and then later Mark Lawrenson and Gary Gillespie at the heart of the Reds' defence.

Hansen made his debut against Derby County at Anfield in September 1977. Terry McDermott scored the winner in a 1-0 victory for Liverpool. He was then in and out of the team for the rest of the 1977/78 season, but was delighted to find himself in the starting line up for the 1978 European Cup final at Wembley. Alan Hansen must have been pinching himself as he

Alan Hansen, a fabulous central defender for Liverpool in the 1980s.

ran out at Wembley that May evening to face Bruges in the greatest of all European club competitions. Kenny Dalglish's winning goal gave the Reds their second consecutive European Cup and Alan Hansen his first major medal in professional football.

Apart from injuries and the odd dip in form, Alan Hansen became virtually an ever-present in the Liverpool defence until he retired from football in 1990. He was selected for Scotland 26 times, although he was surprisingly left out of the Scotland World Cup party in 1986 that participated in the finals.

Hansen took over from Phil Neal as Liverpool skipper in 1985 and led the Reds to four League titles and two FA Cups. By the time he retired at Anfield, Hansen had collected sixteen major winners' medals in domestic and European competitions.

Many thought that he would have made a fine Liverpool manager after his retirement, but the canny Scot had other ideas and decided to develop a career as a BBC soccer pundit instead.

After 604 appearances, scoring 13 goals, Alan Hansen is widely regarded as probably the finest Liverpool central defender of the modern era.

GRAEME SOUNESS

Graeme Souness signed for Liverpool for a £352,000 fee in January 1978. Bob Paisley had seen enough of him strutting his stuff in the colours of Middlesbrough to know that the Edinburgh-born midfield tiger would prove to be a formidable asset to his Liverpool side.

Graeme Souness was skilful with a touch of steel to his play. He possessed a thunderbolt of a shot and was a born leader. It was obvious from the start that he would go on to captain the Reds and he replaced Phil Thompson as skipper at the beginning of 1982. Souness inspired Liverpool to seven major trophies as captain, including the European Cup in 1984.

Graeme Souness's eye for a goal was never more evident than in the 1980/81 European Cup campaign when he hit hat-tricks against Oulu Palloseura and CSKA Sofia in the early rounds of the competition. Souness also popped up with the winner in the 1984 League Cup final replay against Everton at Maine Road.

Apart from goalscoring, Souness possessed the ability to carve open the opposition's defence with a perfectly weighed pass, such as the one that allowed Kenny Dalglish to chip the Bruges goalkeeper and win the European Cup for the Reds in the 1981 Wembley final.

Graeme Souness – has Anfield ever witnessed a better midfield performer in the red shirt of Liverpool?

Graeme Souness took over the mantle in the Liverpool side of the Reds' minder-in-chief when Tommy Smith departed for Swansea City in 1978.

The magnificent Ray Clemence. When he left Liverpool for Spurs in 1981 he was still a world-class goalkeeper.

Souness would exact retribution on any members of the opposition if they dared to take liberties with his Liverpool teammates.

Emlyn Hughes paid Graeme Souness the ultimate compliment of naming him and Kenny Dalglish as the only two world-class players that he played in the same team as during his Anfield career. When you consider that Hughes' Liverpool career was spent in the company of some of the greatest talent that British football has ever seen, that is a compliment indeed.

After 352 appearances for Liverpool, scoring 56 goals, Souness left the Reds in 1984 to join Italian side Sampdoria for a £650,000 transfer fee. His last game for the Reds was the 1984 European Cup final. It was somehow fitting that one of Liverpool's greatest midfielders should bow out at Anfield after winning Europe's major club trophy. Graeme Souness was, after all, one of the ultimate 'winners' in Anfield history.

RAY CLEMENCE

Ray Clemence was signed by Bill Shankly in 1967. The Skegness-born teenager went on to establish himself as the greatest goalkeeper in Liverpool's history. Originally he was Tommy Lawrence's understudy at Anfield, but, after replacing Lawrence in the Reds' line-up in the 1970/71 season, he was Liverpool's no.1 until he signed for Spurs in 1981.

Clemence's golden decade at Anfield was the 1970s, but a European Cup and League Cup double in 1981 meant that the outstanding goalkeeper was still winning silverware at Anfield at the beginning of the 1980s. Ray Clemence was awarded 61 England caps during his professional football career, but this total would surely have doubled if it hadn't been for the brilliance of Peter Shilton.

Bill Shankly gave Ray Clemence his first-team debut against Swansea City in a League Cup tie in 1968, but he had to wait another season to make a Football League appearance for the Reds. Clemence conceded just 22 goals in 41 appearances for Liverpool in the 1970/71 season. Unbelievably, Liverpool still only managed to finish fifth in the table that season, Arsenal ending up as champions. Ray Clemence didn't have to wait long to win a championship medal of his own, Liverpool's 1973 triumph being just the first of five First Division titles he won at Anfield. In Europe, Clemence also collected three European Cup and two UEFA Cup winners' medals, to add to his one FA Cup and one Football League Cup medal haul.

The key to Ray Clemence's superb goalkeeping career with Liverpool, Spurs and England was his fantastic power of concentration. He would often have to go for long periods in a game with little action taking place in the Liverpool goalmouth. When called into action however, Clemence was always alert to danger. He was also an outstanding organiser of the Reds' defence, always keeping his teammates on their toes with his barked-out instructions.

When Ray Clemence signed for Spurs at the start of the 1981/82 season, he was still at his peak as a goalkeeper of world-class ability. Clemence made 470 appearances for Liverpool in a fantastic Anfield career.

DAVID JOHNSON

Liverpool-born David Johnson began his career at Everton and looked an impressive addition to Harry Catterick's Goodison Park squad when he made his debut for the Blues in 1970. Johnson in fact scored on his first appearances

David Johnson

for Everton in four competitions; the Central League, the Football League, the FA Cup and the European Cup.

Unbelievably, Catterick decided to swap Johnson for Ipswich Town's Rod Belfitt in 1972 with no fee being involved. Ipswich boss Bobby Robson could hardly believe his luck as he had just acquired one of the best young strikers in the English game in exchange for a journeyman forward who made just 14 appearances for Everton before being sold off to Sunderland. David Johnson made 136 appearances for Ipswich, between 1972 and 1976, before Bob Paisley paid £200,000 to bring him to Anfield.

David Johnson made his Liverpool debut against Norwich City in August 1976 and scored 3 goals in his first 6 games for the Reds. Johnson failed to establish himself as a first team regular however until the 1978/79 season and even then he only made 26 League appearances. His goal tally of 16 goals was, however, crucial in Liverpool winning the championship that season.

David Johnson was unfortunate to be on the substitute bench for their historic 1977 European Cup victory, but he was in the Liverpool side that beat Real Madrid in the 1981 final in Paris. Johnson won the first of his eight England caps while still at Ipswich Town against Wales in May 1975. Johnson scored twice in a 2-2 draw.

His England career appeared to mirror his Anfield one in that, in some ways, it seemed to be slightly unfulfilled. He was unlucky with injuries at crucial moments in his career, but most professional footballers would give anything to have bagged four League Championship and one European Cup winners' medals as Johnson did in his Anfield days.

David Johnson returned to his original club, Everton in 1982 for a £100,000 transfer fee and scored 4 goals in 40 appearances back at Goodison. He then had spells at Barnsley, Manchester City and Preston, as well as American side Tulsa Roughnecks.

He made 174 appearances for the Reds, scoring 78 goals.

Chapter 2

Liverpool warmed up for the 1982/83 season by once again taking on Spurs at Wembley. The Londoners were FA Cup holders after defeating QPR in the 1982 final and were eager for revenge in the FA Charity Shield. Ian Rush scored the only goal of the game in a 1-0 success for the Reds. It would turn out to be the first of three trophies that Bob Paisley's side would win in the legendary manager's final season at the helm at Anfield.

Craig Johnston, who had been signed for a £575,000 fee back in the summer of 1981, was now beginning to push for a more regular spot in the first-team line-up. In general, however, it was 'as you were' when it came to personnel at Anfield – 'why mend it if it's not broken' seemed to be the Liverpool motto as Paisley's team continued to be the best in the land.

One feature of life at Anfield that never changed was the famous hospitality dished out to visiting managers and their staff when they made their annual visit to play Liverpool. After the game had finished the likes of Brian Clough, Ron Atkinson, Jack Charlton and Bobby Robson would be invited back to the boot room for a post-match drink. Liverpool's hospitality was genuine, but Kenny Dalglish did once reveal that there were also other motives for their generosity with liquid refreshments. Dalglish recalled:

> Ronnie Moran and Roy Evans would sit in their famous hideaway dispensing a little bit of liquid refreshment to visiting managers and coaches, who were always delighted to be invited into Anfield's famous boot room, but it was cunning. All the while Ronnie and Roy were picking up little bits of information about players, perhaps even about tactics. Ronnie and Roy soaked up everything and would then pool the information they had gleaned on Monday morning.

The Liverpool teams of the 1980s were undoubtedly good enough to have swept most teams aside without the help of tongue-loosening booze, but every

Ian Rush in action against Southampton 1982. Southampton's Nick Holmes and Mark Wright are also in the picture.

little helped as the Anfield club continued to dominate English football for the second decade on the run.

The only new signing by Bob Paisley on the eve of the 1982/83 season was Middlesbrough striker David Hodgson for a £450,000 fee. Hodgson started 20 League games for Liverpool in his first season at Anfield, scoring four goals. The following season found Hodgson making just the occasional appearance and eventually he was sold to Sunderland in 1984 for £125,000.

One young player who had been biding his time waiting for an opportunity to break into the Liverpool first team was Steve Nicol. Signed in October 1981 for a £300,000 fee from Ayr United, Nicol would eventually emerge as a fabulous player for the Reds. Nicol could play in practically every position and his goals tally of 45 in 437 games is an example of his ability to find the back of the net on a regular basis. It took Steve Nicol a few seasons to establish himself in the Liverpool first team but, when he did, what an addition to the side he turned out to be.

Liverpool's trophy-winning exploits in the 1982/83 campaign mirrored the previous campaign with the League title and Football League (Milk) Cup finding their way once again into the Anfield trophy cabinet.

The Reds' European Cup dreams ended against Polish side Widzew Lodz. After losing the away leg 2-0, Liverpool put up a determined display of attacking football in the return game at Anfield. Phil Neal, Ian Rush and David Hodgson all scored for the Reds, but the Polish side managed to score two goals of their own to dump Liverpool out of the competition 4-3 on aggregate.

In the FA Cup, Liverpool suffered a shock exit at the hands of Brighton. Brighton went on to reach the 1983 FA Cup final, where they eventually lost 4-0 to Manchester United in a replay after holding them to a 2-2 draw in the first game.

In the First Division, Liverpool held on to their title by a convincing eleven-point margin from Watford. Watford surprised everyone with their adventurous style of play, instigated mainly by future Anfield legend John Barnes.

A crucial element in Liverpool's surge to yet another League title was the outstanding defensive play of Mark Lawrenson and Alan Hansen at the heart of the Reds' defence. Phil Thompson had been enjoying a fine season until hit by injury halfway through the campaign. The outstanding form of Mark Lawrenson in central defence meant that Thompson was unlikely to regain his place in the side and he moved to Sheffield United at the end of the season.

Bruce Grobbelaar had proved himself to be an able replacement for Ray Clemence in the Liverpool goal and although prone to the occasional mistake, for two years on the run he had conceded less goals than any other First Division goalkeeper. When asked his opinion of Grobbelaar, former Arsenal goalkeeper Bob Wilson had no doubts that the Liverpool shot-stopper was top class. Wilson said:

> Bruce was a phenomenon. He'd really rule his box and he wouldn't be afraid to come out 25 to 30 yards to clear the danger. His ability to time that right saved Liverpool time and time again. Occasionally he'd make mistakes, but in the long run he was a hugely successful keeper. People thought he wasn't big enough, but he had an amazing spring. He was a great believer in clearing the first danger and not leaving it to the defender.

The man that Grobbelaar replaced in the Liverpool team, Ray Clemence, also had few doubts that the Durban-born goalkeeper was special. Clemence remarked:

> He's a keeper of exceptional ability; athletic, agile and brilliant at coming to claim crosses. He is also a born entertainer and that is the side of his game that

The Liverpool team that beat Manchester United 2-1 after extra time to win the 1983 League (Milk) Cup final at Wembley. From left to right, back row: Lawrenson, Fairclough, Hansen, Whelan, Rush, Grobbelaar, Paisley (manager). Front row: Johnston, Dalglish, Neal, Souness, Lee, A. Kennedy.

attracts the publicity and gets him into trouble. With a team like Liverpool the goalkeeper can often be out of action for long periods. When this happens to Bruce he seems to feel he has to do something out of the ordinary to justify his existence, but there's no need for it.

Up front for Liverpool the Dalglish/Rush partnership was now in full bloom and the Welsh international scored 24 goals in 34 League games. Kenny Dalglish was an ever-present in the Reds' League campaign and netted 18 goals in 42 appearances. Dalglish and Rush were a dream team in attack for the Reds during this period. Ian Rush once said that Dalglish set up over half his goals for Liverpool and the compliment was returned when the Scot named Rush as his best ever partner at Anfield. Dalglish remarked:

We complimented each other well. He was easily the best partner I had at Liverpool. We also had another role which people often don't give us credit for. Bob Paisley told us that we were his first line of defence. When the opposition had the ball Rushie and I worked hard to allow our midfield or defence to regroup.

The Liverpool side that romped to the League title in 1983 might have been sprinkled with world-class performers, but it was always drilled into them that the team came first. 'There has never been any room for prima-donnas at Liverpool', Ian Rush once declared. 'Players like Dalglish and Souness were renowned throughout the whole world, yet they were treated no different than the rest.'

Graeme Souness had enjoyed another fine season at Anfield, leading the side to glory in the League and League Cup. Souness had taken over the captaincy of the side in the 1981/82 campaign and to Bob Paisley he was the heartbeat

Graeme Souness, Kenny Dalglish and Alan Hansen hold the League (Milk) Cup aloft after Liverpool beat Manchester United 2-1 in 1983.

of the team. Paisley said of Souness, 'Make no mistake about it, Graeme Souness is a very good player, but more than anything he is a leader. He thrives on responsibility and is a born winner.'

Ian Rush said that it was Souness who kept him psyched up throughout the whole game and, if he needed it, it was the fearsome Scot who would give him a rollicking as well to keep him on his game.

Liverpool's success in the 1983 League Cup final against Manchester United gave Bob Paisley's side the perfect opportunity to make an unprecedented gesture to honour their boss who was retiring at the end of the season. Goals from Alan Kennedy and Ronnie Whelan gave Liverpool a 2-1 victory over United after extra time. The players decided to ask Paisley to climb the steps to the Royal Box at Wembley and collect the trophy on behalf of the team. Liverpool had just become the first club to win the League Cup in three successive seasons and the icing on the cake was the sight of their great manager holding the trophy aloft. 'That 1983 League Cup victory was special', said Kenny Dalglish:

> It gave us the chance to honour Bob in his final season as manager. We decided to let him collect the Cup as a mark of respect for the man. He loved it. I also remember him walking down the tunnel at Anfield holding the League Championship trophy. It was sad to see Bob leave, but he went out holding trophies.

RAY KENNEDY

Ray Kennedy was Bill Shankly's last signing for Liverpool before he retired in the summer of 1974. The £180,000 fee was money well spent and the former Arsenal striker was converted by Shankly's successor, Bob Paisley, into one of the finest midfielders in Anfield's history. Kennedy's great days at Liverpool were undoubtedly in the mid-1970s, but he also picked up several winners' medals in the early 1980s.

Ray Kennedy was expected to shine at Anfield as a goalscoring forward. He had been a key figure in Arsenal's double-winning side of the 1970/71 season and scored many vital goals alongside John Radford in the Gunners' attack. Bob Paisley decided to give Kennedy a different role in the Reds' line-up, playing behind Toshack and Keegan in the all-conquering side of the 1970s.

With his eye for goal, Ray Kennedy scored many a vital strike for Liverpool from his midfield berth, most notably in Europe when he hit the equaliser

Ray Kennedy

against Bayern Munich in the 1981 European Cup semi-final. Liverpool looked to be heading out of the competition when Ray Kennedy popped up with a late equaliser against the Germans to send the Reds through on the away goals rule.

Playing mainly in midfield, Kennedy's tally of 72 goals in 384 appearances for the Reds makes impressive reading. On the international scene Ray Kennedy made 17 appearances for England, but, like many Liverpool internationals of the era, he performed better in the colours of his club than the white of the national side. Liverpool's style of play suited him down to the ground and their midfield formation of Souness, Case, McDermott and Kennedy did not lose many battles during the 1970s and 1980s.

Ray Kennedy won three European Cups in the red shirt of Liverpool, their 1981 1-0 victory over Real Madrid being his last. There were also five League Championships, one UEFA Cup and a League Cup medal to add to his medal tally before he departed for Swansea City in December 1982. By that time Kennedy's appearances in the Reds' first team had virtually come to an end. Ray Kennedy's contribution to one of the finest eras in Liverpool's history will, however, never be forgotten.

PHIL NEAL

Born in Irchester, Northants, Phil Neal was one of the most accomplished full-backs to ever pull on the red shirt of Liverpool. Bob Paisley plucked Neal from the relative obscurity of lower-league football at Northampton Town

Phil Neal

for a £65,000 fee in October 1974 and gave him his debut against Everton a few weeks later.

Liverpool chief scout, Geoff Twentyman, a man who brought an abundance of talented players to Anfield after giving the Liverpool hierarchy his personal recommendations, watched Phil Neal several times and told Bob Paisley to snap him up.

Neal adjusted well to the step up in class and kept his place in the Liverpool defence for the rest of the 1974/75 season. Phil Neal could operate at either full-back position, but after a while he made the right-back spot his own.

Phil Neal soon came to the attention of the England selectors and made his international debut against Wales at the Racecourse Ground in Wrexham in 1976. Neal certainly felt at home in the England set-up, with Ray Clemence, Phil Thompson, Kevin Keegan and Ray Kennedy all in the side that beat Wales 2-1. Neal went on to accumulate 50 England caps between 1976 and 1983.

One of Phil Neal's great strengths as a defender was his excellent positional play and he also very rarely picked up injuries. Between December 1974 and October 1983 Neal had a remarkable run of 366 unbroken appearances for the Reds in First Division games.

Phil Neal was also an excellent spot-kick specialist for Liverpool with most of his 59 goals for the Reds coming from penalties. Phil Neal's most memorable penalty for Liverpool was undoubtedly the kick that sealed the Reds' 3-1 victory against Borussia Moenchengladbach in the 1977 European Cup final in Rome.

By the time Phil Neal left Liverpool in 1985 to become player-manager at Bolton Wanderers, he had made 633 appearances for the Reds. Only Ian Callaghan, Emlyn Hughes, Ray Clemence and Ian Rush had played more times for the Reds. Phil Neal's medal haul at Liverpool, which includes four European Cup victories and seven League Championship successes, also makes impressive reading.

TERRY MCDERMOTT

Terry McDermott was born in the Kirkby district of Liverpool and signed for Liverpool from Newcastle United for a £170,000 fee in 1974. Bob Paisley had taken quite a shine to McDermott after witnessing the midfielder's performances for Newcastle during the early 1970s.

McDermott was handed his Liverpool debut against Everton in a 0-0 draw at Goodison Park in November 1974. Initially McDermott took a little time to settle into the Liverpool set-up and made just 15 League appearances in

Terry McDermott

his first season at the club. The following year's campaign saw the midfielder making just nine League appearances and it was not until the 1977/78 season that Terry McDermott finally became a permanent fixture in the Liverpool side. Bob Paisley gave the midfielder a run in the side in the final games of the previous campaign and he rewarded the Liverpool boss with the opening goal in the 1977 European Cup final against Borussia Moenchengladbach.

Terry McDermott had picked up a League Championship and European Cup medal without really feeling that he had fully proved himself at Anfield. By the late 1970s and early 1980s, McDermott was being touted as one of the finest attacking midfielders in the English game. He was voted Footballer of the Year in 1980 and was also an England regular.

Anfield commentators claim that it was the arrival of Graeme Souness in 1978 that really helped in McDermott finally realising his potential at Liverpool. McDermott scored many notable goals in his Anfield career, 75 in 310 appearances, but his magnificent header in the Reds' 7-0 rout of Spurs in 1978 is regarded as his finest. McDermott began the move in his own penalty area and then ran the length of the pitch to finish off a fabulous flowing move between several members of the Liverpool team.

By the time Terry McDermott left Liverpool to rejoin Newcastle in 1982, he had won a bagful of honours, including a European Cup, a League Championship and two League Cup winners' medals gained at the beginning of the 1980s.

SAMMY LEE

It is sometimes overlooked just how vital Liverpool-born Sammy Lee was to the Reds' success in the 1980s. Standing at just 5ft 7ins, Lee was a tough, competitive performer for Liverpool throughout his career. He was strong in the tackle and was blessed with an abundance of stamina.

Sammy Lee made his Liverpool debut in a 1-1 draw at Southampton in April 1979. He also appeared against Nottingham Forest a few days later as a substitute. The following season saw Lee make just seven more appearances for the Reds in the League, but all the time he was learning his trade.

By the 1980/81 campaign Sammy Lee was virtually an ever-present in the Liverpool side that finished a disappointing fifth in the League, but managed to win the Football League Cup with a 2-1 victory over West Ham in the replay at Villa Park after the Wembley final finished at 1-1.

Sammy Lee's fine form in the Liverpool engine room soon caught the eye of the England manager and he was selected to make his international debut against Greece in Salonika towards the end of 1982. Goals from Tony Woodcock, with two, and Sammy Lee himself, gave England a fine 3-0 victory. Lee went on to make 14 international appearances between 1982 and 1984.

The highlights of Sammy Lee's Liverpool career were undoubtedly the European Cup victories of 1981 and 1984. Lee also won four League Championship medals

Sammy Lee

during his Anfield career and four Football League Cup winners' medals. His goal tally of 19 in 286 games was not in the Souness, Case, McDermott or Ray Kennedy ratio, but Lee was never an attacking midfielder in the style of the four players listed. He would often be found covering at full-back when the likes of Phil Neal and Alan Kennedy had taken up attacking positions.

Sammy Lee looked as though he had all the makings to emulate the likes of Ian Callaghan and be at Anfield well into his thirties. In his mid-twenties his high level of performance did begin to dip, however, and Craig Johnston found himself selected in the Liverpool side playing the type of role that Sammy Lee had performed so admirably for the past five years.

Lee signed for QPR in 1986. He also had spells at Osasuna, Southampton and Bolton Wanderers.

Alan Kennedy

ALAN KENNEDY

Alan Kennedy was born in Sunderland and joined Newcastle United as an apprentice in 1971. He appeared against Liverpool in the 1974 FA Cup final and Bob Paisley liked the look of the tough tackling full-back. Kennedy was similar in style to Gerry Bryne, the 1960s full-back who was such a vital part of the Reds' success in that decade, although obviously not as hard in the tackle – very few were!

Alan Kennedy was purchased by Bob Paisley for a £330,000 transfer fee from Newcastle in August 1978 and made his debut against QPR in a 2–1 victory at Anfield. Always keen to attack, Alan Kennedy took little time to show the Liverpool fans that he was a left-back who could score vital goals and scored the Reds' third in a 3-0 win at Birmingham early in the new season.

Alan Kennedy ended his first season at Liverpool with a League Championship medal to show for his endeavours. It was the first of five League Championship winning teams that he would feature in during his Liverpool career. Kennedy also went on to win four Football League Cup winners' medals and two European Cups before leaving Anfield in 1985.

The highlights of his Liverpool career were obviously playing in two European Cup winning sides and in 1981, in the final in Paris against Real Madrid, it was Kennedy who popped up with the winner in Liverpool's 1-0 victory.

Given the quality of Alan Kennedy's form for Liverpool, the fact that he only won two England international caps was something of a mystery. He was selected to play against Northern Ireland in April 1984, a game that England won 1-0 through a Tony Woodcock goal. His only other international appearance was against Wales a few weeks later. England lost that game 1-0 and Alan Kennedy's international career came to an end. The fact that Kenny Sansom had by now been restored to the England set-up could have had something to do with Kennedy's meagre amount of international appearances.

Alan Kennedy left Liverpool in 1985 to join his home-town club Sunderland – the fee was £100,000.

Chapter 3

The start of the 1983/84 season saw Joe Fagan at the helm at Liverpool. Fagan had been a coach at Anfield since 1958 and when Bill Shankly arrived at the club a year later he was happy to keep the former Manchester City defender on the backroom staff.

Joe Fagan had been Bob Paisley's assistant since 1974 and his appointment meant that continuity at Anfield was retained. The players were delighted that Fagan was the new boss. Liverpool captain at the time, Graeme Souness, remarked, 'Joe and Bob Paisley had been so close for so many years that we hardly noticed the difference. We used the same hotels, the same training methods and things ticked along very much the same.'

When it came to their temperament however, there were slight differences between Paisley and Fagan. 'Bob Paisley would occasionally lose his temper, but not half as much as Joe Fagan, and when Joe does, he really goes wild.' Liverpool striker Ian Rush once remarked.

In general, however, Fagan was a popular and well respected figure at Anfield. His first game in charge saw them lose 2-0 to Manchester United in the Charity Shield. After that it was mainly success all the way for Liverpool and their new boss.

Liverpool did make a slightly stuttering start to their League campaign with early season's defeats against Manchester United and Sunderland. By the start of November, however, they had moved to the top of the table. An impressive 3-0 win over Everton at Anfield, with new £200,000 striker Mick Robinson scoring one of the goals, put the seal on a fine run of victories for the Reds.

Prior to their derby triumph, Ian Rush had bagged five goals in a 6-0 thrashing of Luton Town at Anfield. Former Liverpool great Kevin Keegan was a spectator at this game and told the press, 'That's how football should be played. Liverpool seem to get better and better like a good wine.'

Liverpool's main challengers for the 1983/84 League Championship turned out to be Southampton, Nottingham Forest, Manchester United and QPR. Apart from a slight stutter in March, the Reds remained at the top of the table from November until clinching the title with a 5-0 victory over Coventry and then a 0-0 draw at Notts County early in May.

Ian Rush had enjoyed a fantastic season when it came to goalscoring and he netted four of the goals at Coventry. His final tally of 32 goals in 41 League games was quite phenomenal and bettered the great Roger Hunt's 31 in 41 League appearances in Liverpool's title-winning 1963/64 season.

Liverpool did have the odd blip during the 1983/84 campaign such as their exit against Brighton in the early rounds of the FA Cup for the second consecutive season. In general, however, it was success all the way and new manager, Joe Fagan, must have been left thinking that this manager lark was not really as hard as it was cracked up to be.

Apart from success in the League, Liverpool became only the third club in history after Huddersfield and Arsenal to win three League titles in a row. The Reds also tasted success in the European Cup and League Cup.

Liverpool full-back Alan Kennedy had been a key member of the Reds' team that had completed a hat-trick of League Championship victories. Kennedy was delighted to be a member of such an outstanding Liverpool side, but thought that the other teams at the top of the table might have made it more difficult for the Reds. Kennedy said, 'We battled on and we won it. There's nothing better than winning the League. I do think that Manchester United, QPR and Southampton might have pushed us harder though.'

Liverpool's run through to the 1984 Football League (Milk) Cup final involved some hard fought victories. Their victory over Fulham only came after extra time, after three nail- biting encounters. It then took two games to get past Birmingham and in the next round Sheffield Wednesday also took Fagan's team to a replay. Liverpool could easily have gone out against Sheffield Wednesday and were saved by a late Phil Neal equaliser from the penalty spot. Neal was proving himself to be quite an expert with spot-kicks and the importance of his penalty against Sheffield Wednesday caused him to remark, 'The following morning I woke up and realised what it could have cost the club if I'd missed the penalty against Sheffield Wednesday. It's probably the most important penalty that I've ever taken.'

Liverpool reached the final of the League Cup after a 4-2 on aggregate win over Walsall in the semi-finals. Liverpool's opponents in the final were Merseyside neighbours Everton. It was the first time that Liverpool and Everton had met in a major final and Joe Fagan knew that the Reds would have a tough task against a rejuvenated Goodison Park outfit.

Ian Rush in action against his Wales teammate Kevin Ratcliffe in the 1984 League (Milk) Cup final at Wembley. Liverpool won the trophy 1-0 in the replay at Maine Road after the first game ended in a 0-0 draw.

As Merseyside converged on Wembley for the League Cup final, players from both teams were taken aback by the sight of Everton and Liverpool fans walking to the ground together. Kenny Dalglish recalled, 'Both sets of fans were unbelievable. I saw a father walking along with his two sons, one wearing red the other blue. That was a lovely sight, which showed how football rivalry should be.' Dalglish had served his football apprenticeship at Celtic and to witness the contrast between Merseyside football fans and their Glasgow counterparts, where an atmosphere of hatred pervades Celtic against Rangers encounters was a refreshing sight for the Liverpool star.

Adrian Heath of Everton once proclaimed that it might have become known as the friendly final off the pitch, but on the field of play it was far from friendly. From the kick-off the tackles flew in and even thirty minutes of extra time failed to find a goal as the first all-Merseyside final ended 0-0. Liverpool won the replay at Maine Road 1-0 through a Graeme Souness goal. The Evertonians were heart broken, but the fact that they now had a team that were on the rise gave them supreme optimism for the future. Howard Kendall's team had now emerged as the only true competition that Liverpool would come up against for the rest of the decade in the English game.

Everton's Graeme Sharp is tracked by Liverpool's Graeme Souness and Craig Johnston in the 1984 League (Milk) Cup final at Wembley. The match ended in a 0-0 draw.

The victorious Liverpool team celebrate their League (Milk) Cup victory over Everton after a replay at Maine Road in March 1984. Graeme Souness scored the only goal of the game. From left to right, back row: A. Kennedy, Robinson, Grobbelaar, Rush, Hansen, Dalglish. Front row: Lee, Souness, Neal, Johnston, Whelan, Lawrenson.

With two trophies in the bag Liverpool had also fought their way through to the final of the 1984 European Cup. Wins against BK Odense, Athletic Bilbao, Benfica and Dynamo Bucharest in the semi finals put Fagan's side in the final where they would play Roma. The game was to take place in the Olympic Stadium in Rome. With home advantage, the Italian champions were clear favourites. Speaking before the game Liverpool central defender, Alan Hansen said, 'It would be fantastic if we can win the treble. We've got to go to Rome, but if there's one team who can do it, it's this team.'

When Liverpool ran out to a cauldron of noise to face Roma in the 1984 European Cup final the experience of Fagan's side really came into its own. Showing little sign of nerves Liverpool soaked up early Roma pressure before

The Liverpool team that won the 1984 European Cup final against Roma in Italy. Liverpool won the cup 4-2 on penalties after the game ended in a 1-1 draw after extra time. From left to right, back row: Grobbelaar, A. Kennedy, Dalglish, Lawrenson, Hansen, Rush. Front row: Neal, Lee, Souness, Johnston, Whelan.

Phil Neal put the Reds into the lead. A poor clearance from the Roma defence rebounded off Ian Rush into the path of Phil Neal who stroked the ball home. Pruzzo then grabbed an equaliser for Roma to send the home fans delirious. Pruzzo's goal came just before half-time and the remaining forty-five minutes failed to produce a winner. The dreaded penalty shoot-out now came into play. Liverpool boss Joe Fagan revealed after the game that he had had his team practicing spot-kicks in the days before the final and that his reserve team had come out on top on every occasion. When it came to the real thing Liverpool held their nerve to come out as 1984 European Cup winners. After Nicol had blazed Liverpool's first spot-kick over the bar their chances looked slim. Di Bartolomei then gave Roma the lead. Neal scored for Liverpool, who were relieved to witness Conti miss for Roma. Souness and Rush then slotted home their spot-kicks.

Ian Rush and Craig Johnston hold the European Cup after Liverpool's victory over Roma in 1984.

The Liverpool team celebrate their 1984 European Cup victory over Roma in Italy.

In between Liverpool's successful efforts Righetti had scored for Roma. Graziani then stepped up for Roma and, to unnerve the Italian, Bruce Grobbelaar began to wobble his legs. Graziani was clearly put off and his shot flew over the bar. If Alan Kennedy could convert the next penalty kick the European Cup would be returning to Anfield. The Liverpool full-back duly stepped up and smashed the ball home. Liverpool had won their fourth European Cup and Joe Fagan had achieved a fantastic treble of trophies in just his first season as manager. The Liverpool fans in the stadium and thousands more back home on Merseyside celebrated late into the night.

It was Liverpool captain Graeme Souness's last game for the club before joining Italian team Sampdoria. To him it was the pinnacle of his career at Anfield. Souness later reflected:

> That 1984 European Cup final win was my highlight. It was my last game for Liverpool. The last time that I kicked a ball for them was scoring a penalty in the shoot out. The last thing I did as captain was to lift the European Cup aloft. I've got fantastic memories of being a player at Liverpool but that was my real highlight. It was a fantastic time to be a player at Liverpool because we knew we were better than anyone that we were going to play against.

Alan Hansen said, 'That 1984 side just had something about it. In Rome it was awesome. The side had a resilience that saw it through difficult situations and difficult matches.'

Former Reds' captain Phil Thompson, speaking about the 1984 Liverpool side, said, 'That was a team in the great Liverpool tradition. They could soak up huge amounts of punishment away from home and then take you apart at Anfield.' When the dust had settled the victorious Liverpool side returned back to their dressing room in the Olympic Stadium and reflected on what they had just achieved. Kenny Dalglish recalled Joe Fagan's reactions when the door to the dressing room was closed to the outside world: 'Joe just stood there in the middle of the room and let out a huge cry of delight. It was unfair that we had to play Roma on their own ground, so victory was all the sweeter.'

BRUCE GROBBELAAR

Bruce Grobbelaar was a fine goalkeeper for Liverpool during the 1980s. A mixture of sheer brilliance, and at other times slightly erratic, Grobbelaar

Bruce Grobbelaar

played 610 times for the Reds and you don't make that number of appearances at Anfield if you are not blessed with a special talent.

Bob Paisley paid £250,000 to Vancouver Whitecaps in March 1981. Grobbelaar had also had a spell on loan at Crewe during the 1979/80 season. Paisley knew that the Durban-born goalkeeper had a hard act to follow at Anfield, replacing the brilliant Ray Clemence after he decided to join Spurs. Grobbelaar was never lacking in confidence throughout his Anfield career and the Liverpool boss had no qualms about selecting him right from the start of the 1981/82 season.

Grobbelaar made his debut in the Reds' 1-0 away defeat at Wolves on the opening day of the new season and was an ever-present throughout Liverpool's title-winning campaign that finished with the goalkeeper winning the first of his six League Championship medals.

Bruce Grobbelaar represented Zimbabwe 15 times in international matches and won three FA Cups, three League Cups and one European Cup to add to his League Championship medal haul.

His wobbling legs routine in the penalty shoot-out against Roma in the 1984 European Cup final is still talked about to this day. Grobbelaar knew he had to do something to put off Graziani as he ran up to take a penalty, and wobbling his legs certainly paid dividends as the Roma striker missed with his spot-kick. Jerzy Dudek copied Grobbelaar's routine in the penalty shoot-out that saw Liverpool defeat AC Milan in the 2005 European Cup final.

Bruce Grobbelaar left Liverpool in 1994 to join Southampton on a free transfer. His career had been quite spectacular at times and never at any stage boring. There were several bust ups with his own teammates and well-publicised howlers defending the Liverpool goal. Some regarded him as nothing more than a clown who was lucky to play behind brilliant defenders that gave the opposition very few scoring opportunities. In the history of Liverpool Football Club, however, only Callaghan, Hughes, Clemence, Rush, Neal and Smith played more games for the Reds, a fact that tells you everything about Grobbelaar's outstanding goalkeeping ability.

CRAIG JOHNSTON

Craig Johnston was born in Johannesburg, South Africa. His parents were British and he played for Lake McQuarrie and Sydney City Football Clubs before paying his own way to England in an attempt to break into the Football League. Middlesbrough gave him a three-month trial and he turned professional with them in 1978. Bob Paisley paid £650,000 for Johnston before the start of the 1981/82 season.

Craig Johnston made his Liverpool debut away at Wolves on the opening day of the 1981/82 campaign, coming on as a substitute for Ray Kennedy. The Reds lost the game 1-0 and Johnston was not given his full First Division debut until a few months later. He took Terry McDermott's midfield place against Manchester City on Boxing Day in Liverpool's 3-1 defeat.

Craig Johnston

Johnston's first goal for Liverpool came the following March away to Everton. Liverpool's 3–1 victory at Goodison went a long way to helping them win the championship that season and Craig Johnston retained his place in the side for the rest of the season.

Craig Johnston went on to win five League titles, two League Cups and the FA Cup during his Anfield career. He was also in the Liverpool side that beat Roma in the 1984 European Cup final.

Johnston was popular with the Anfield faithful who could see similarities with former Kop favourite Kevin Keegan in Johnston's all-action style of play.

David Hodgson – a £450,000 buy from Middlesbrough in 1982. Hodgson won a League title medal in the 1982/83 season, making 23 appearances for the Reds in their successful Championship campaign.

Like Keegan, he was supremely fit and had a fantastic burst of speed that set up many a goalscoring opportunity for the likes of Rush and Dalglish.

Craig Johnston was, above all, a grafter who never knew when he was beaten and his work rate for the Liverpool cause sometimes tended to be undervalued in the Reds' fantastic trophy-winning years of the 1980s. Johnston was always likely to pop up with vital goals for the Reds, such as the crucial third in Liverpool's 3-1 victory over Everton in the 1986 FA Cup final. Craig Johnston scored 39 goals for Liverpool in his 260 appearances.

Craig Johnston's last appearance for Liverpool came in the 1988 FA Cup final which the Reds lost 1-0 to Wimbledon. He then unexpectedly decided to return to Australia to care for his seriously ill sister. He also took up other interests such as photography and television work.

MARK LAWRENSON

Preston-born Mark Lawrenson turned out to be a fabulous signing for the Reds when Bob Paisley paid Brighton £900,000 for his services before

Mark Lawrenson

the start of the 1981/82 season. His central defensive partnership with Alan Hansen was a vital part of Liverpool's success in the 1980s.

Liverpool knew they were getting a top-class performer when they broke their own transfer record to bring him to Anfield, but Lawrenson's displays at the heart of the Reds' defence were out of the top drawer. Lawrenson was versatile as well and was equally happy at full-back or in a midfield role for Paisley's team.

Although Lawrenson developed into a player who would have been a valuable addition to the England side, he decided to plump for the Republic of Ireland when they came calling in 1977. He went on to play for the country where his father was born 38 times between 1977 and 1987.

Mark Lawrenson was a member of the 1984 European Cup-winning team and also won five League Championships, three League Cups and one FA Cup winners' medal in his Liverpool career.

Bob Paisley gave Lawrenson his Liverpool debut against Wolves at the start of the 1981/82 season. Initially he played at left-back, but an injury to Phil Thompson at the beginning of December in the 1982/83 campaign led to Lawrenson playing as Alan Hansen's central defensive partner in the Reds' line-up. The defensive pairing of Lawrenson and Hansen proved an immediate success and Phil Thompson never really regained his place at the heart of the Liverpool defence. Throughout the mid-1980s the Lawrenson/Hansen partnership continued to be a nightmare for opposition attacks to try and pierce and at their peak they must have been amongst the best central defensive pairing in European football.

Mark Lawrenson's final season at Liverpool was 1987/88 when the Reds romped to yet another First Division title. An offer was then made to Lawrenson to become manager at Oxford United. A serious injury to his Achilles tendon had led to him missing a great deal of his final campaign at Anfield and his failure to make a full recovery saw him moving into football management. After brief spells at Oxford and Peterborough, Mark Lawrenson then decided that football management was not for him and he moved into radio and television broadcasting work.

Chapter 4

Joe Fagan's first season in the manager's chair at Liverpool was one of glittering success. His second ended in tragedy and tears.

As reigning English and European champions, Liverpool began the 1984/85 campaign looking for more of the same. Everton had served notice in the previous season that Howard Kendal had put together a team that were now capable of giving their city rivals a run for their money when it came to the battle for domestic honours.

The departure of Graeme Souness in the summer to Sampdoria was a blow to Joe Fagan, but great players had departed from Anfield before and the trophies had still kept on coming. The talented Danish international Jan Molby had been brought in for a £200,000 fee from Ajax and he would eventually turn out to be a great purchase for the Reds. The Leicester midfielder Kevin MacDonald was also signed for £400,000 in an effort to plug the gap left by Souness's departure. It was not until the highly skilful and combative Steve McMahon was signed, the following season, that Liverpool felt they now had an adequate replacement for the outstanding Souness.

The first sign that the 1984/85 campaign would not be an easy ride for Liverpool came in the Charity Shield when FA Cup holders Everton achieved a rare victory over the men from Anfield. A Bruce Grobbelaar own goal gave the Blues a 1-0 victory. Outside of Merseyside, winning this particular Charity Shield encounter was of little consequence. There could be little doubt, however, that Everton had struck a psychological blow before the League campaign had even started.

A fabulous Graeme Sharp goal then gave Everton a 1-0 victory at Anfield in the October 1984 derby, a defeat which left Liverpool sitting in eighteenth place in the table. The balance of power on Merseyside was starting to swing towards Goodison Park for the time being. Howard Kendall's team won the title at a canter with five games of the season still to be played. Liverpool made

Above: *Liverpool's boot room boys during the brief but successful Fagan era at Anfield. From left to right: Chris Lawler, Roy Evans, Joe Fagan (manager) and Ronnie Moran celebrate their team's European Cup victory in 1984.*

Left: *From left to right: Ronnie Moran, Roy Evans and Joe Fagan at the World Club Championship held in Tokyo in 1984. Liverpool lost 1-0 to Argentina's Independiente.*

up ground to finish runners-up, but to finish thirteen points behind the Blues still came as a bitter blow.

In Europe, however, Fagan's team looked highly likely to retain the European Cup. Victories over Lech Poznan, Benfica, Austria Vienna and Panathinaikos put them into their second consecutive European Cup final. Juventus, the champions of Italy, had also battled their way through to the final to be played in Brussels. In the FA Cup there was also the prospect of a second consecutive all-Merseyside final at Wembley, but defeat in a semi-final replay at Maine Road sent Manchester United through to face Everton.

The 1984/85 season had already witnessed one end of season tragedy on the 11 May with fifty-six people losing their lives at Bradford City's Valley Parade. Bradford supporters had flocked to the ground in their thousands to celebrate their heroes' Third Division title triumph in the last game of the campaign against Lincoln City. Just before the half-time interval a fire started in the main stand and fifty-six died with many more badly injured.

Liverpool's European Cup final took place two weeks later on the 29 May at the Heysel Stadium in Brussels. As with Valley Parade, the Heysel Stadium was also another run-down, dilapidated sports venue and should never have been selected to hold a European Cup final. Trouble between Liverpool and Juventus fans had started hours before the match had even started and during one bout of mayhem, Juventus fans, fleeing from a charging group of Liverpool supporters, found themselves crushed under a collapsed brick wall. In the ensuing chaos fans were trampled on and crushed and thirty-nine Juventus fans lost their lives with over 400 more injured.

On the advice of the police the game took place and Juventus won the trophy 1-0, but few cared. Football was of little importance at that moment in time. After an enquiry by UEFA all English clubs were banned from European competitions indefinitely with Liverpool handed an additional three-year ban once English teams were allowed back in. The sight of a tearful Joe Fagan arriving back at Speke Airport, Liverpool, after the Heysel tragedy stayed long in the memory of Liverpool fans, many of whom found it hard to come to terms with what they had just witnessed in the name of sport.

Joe Fagan confirmed that his brief term as Liverpool manager had come to an end and, somewhat surprisingly, Kenny Dalglish was named as the new boss of Anfield.

JAN MOLBY

Jan Molby signed for Liverpool in August 1984 from Dutch team Ajax. The fee that Joe Fagan paid was £200,000 which turned out to be quite a bargain. Molby was a brilliant midfield performer for the Reds in their memorable double triumph of 1985/86. Born in Kolding, Denmark, Molby was signed by Ajax from Danish amateur football while still a teenager. Joe Fagan gave Molby his Liverpool debut against Norwich City at the start of the 1984/85 season. He made just 19 League appearances for the Reds in his first season at the club.

It was the following year that Anfield really saw the best of Jan Molby as he played a vital part in helping the Reds achieve success in both the First Division and FA Cup. The skilful midfielder was at the heart of many of Liverpool's outstanding displays during the momentous season and he also chipped in with 18 goals in League and cup competitions.

Jan Molby

Molby was something of a specialist at free-kicks and rarely missed from the penalty spot. Although Liverpool finished out of the honours the following season, Molby still had a fine campaign for the Reds, scoring 7 goals in 34 appearances. Injury virtually wiped out Jan Molby's Liverpool first-team appearances during the 1987/88 and 1988/89 seasons, but he picked up another League Championship medal the following year and an FA Cup winners' medal in the 1991/92 season.

Jan Molby's Liverpool career never really hit the dizzy heights of the 1985/86 campaign throughout the rest of his Anfield stay. Problems with injuries, his weight and a three-month prison stretch in October 1988 curtailed his expected emergence as one of the greatest Liverpool midfielders of all time. He recovered well from the indignity of a prison sentence to come back and win further honours in the red shirt of Liverpool. After 251 appearances for the Reds, Jan Molby had spells at Barnsley and Swansea before becoming player-manager at the Welsh club in 1996.

Jan Molby had magnificent spells during his Anfield career, but he just falls short when it comes to him being regarded as one of the all-time Liverpool greats.

JOHN WARK

Glasgow-born John Wark was signed by Joe Fagan from Ipswich Town for a £450,000 fee in March 1984. Graeme Souness was on his way to Sampdoria at the end of the season and Fagan hoped that Wark would prove an able replacement for Liverpool's midfield supremo.

When it came to goalscoring, Wark's tally of 42 goals in 102 League appearances was an outstanding contribution for a midfielder. The trouble was that John Wark spent far too much time on the treatment table after a fine 1984/85 season at Anfield, during which he scored 18 goals in 40 League games.

Joe Fagan gave Wark his League debut against Watford at Vicarage Road. Wark scored in a 2-0 victory in March 1984. The Scot, however, only managed to play in nine games in what turned out to be a title-winning season for Liverpool and he did not qualify for a medal. During Liverpool's next championship winning campaign of 1985/86, John Wark played only nine League games and once again missed out on a winners' medal.

Although Wark was a talented performer, his spell at Liverpool was a catalogue of missed opportunities with failure to participate in the historic FA Cup-winning victory of 1986 through a broken leg and also missing out on European Cup glory after the horrors of the Heysel Stadium tragedy in

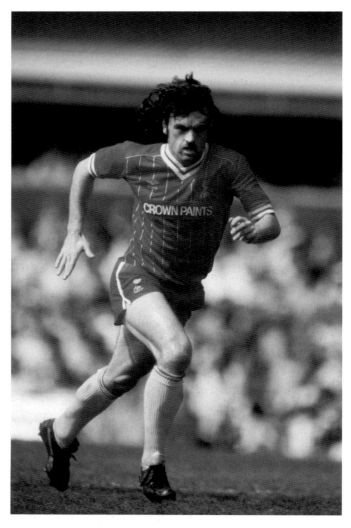

John Wark

1985. John Wark's injury problems also led to him missing out on travelling to Mexico with Scotland for the 1986 World Cup finals.

In January 1988 John Wark was offered the chance to return to the scene of former glories when Ipswich Town made Kenny Dalglish a £100,000 offer for the midfielder's services. Wark jumped at the chance to return to Portman Road and had three happy seasons playing for Ipswich before joining Middlesbrough in 1990. Wark returned to Ipswich Town a year later.

If John Wark had been luckier with injuries his Anfield career could have turned out to have been a lot more memorable than ultimately it was.

STEVE NICOL

Steve Nicol was a magnificent servant to Liverpool Football Club after Bob Paisley captured him from Ayr United for a £300,000 fee in October 1981.

Steve Nicol was born in Irvine, Ayrshire, and joined his local side in 1979. He made 70 appearances for Ayr before joining the Reds and after proving himself in the Liverpool Central League side, Paisley gave him a first-team opportunity against Birmingham City in the second game of the 1982/83 season. Nicol played just one more League game that season, but the following year he was selected by Bob Paisley on a more regular basis.

Steve Nicol

He picked up his first Anfield silverware after helping the Reds to win the League Championship in 1984 and he also appeared in that year's European Cup final. He came on for Craig Johnston against Roma and, despite missing a penalty in the shoot-out at the end of extra time, Nicol was relieved to see his teammates all tuck home their spot-kick efforts.

Steve Nicol won four League titles, three FA Cups and 27 Scotland caps during his Liverpool career. He was also voted Footballer of the Year in 1989. Signed primarily to play at full-back, Nicol proved himself to be one of the most versatile players in Liverpool's history. He was equally as good in defence or midfield and the fact that he scored 45 goals in 453 appearances tells you that he knew how to find the net as well. Steve Nicol once even scored a hat-trick for the Reds in a 4-1 away victory over Newcastle United in September 1987, John Aldridge scoring the other Liverpool goal.

After eleven seasons of priceless service, Liverpool allowed Steve Nicol to join Notts County on a free transfer in 1994. He spent two seasons in Nottingham, making 34 appearances before joining Sheffield Wednesday at the start of the 1995/96 season. He played 19 times for Wednesday before his playing days in English football came to an end.

Steve Nicol's outstanding performances in the red shirt of Liverpool made the £300,000 paid for him look to be one of the greatest bargain buys of all time.

KEVIN MACDONALD

Inverness-born Kevin MacDonald was signed by Joe Fagan from Leicester City for a £400,000 fee in November 1980. He had been brought to Leicester for a £26,000 fee from Inverness Caledonian in 1980.

MacDonald developed into one of the most sought after midfield players in the English game during his time at Filbert Street and was instrumental in enabling Leicester to win promotion back into the First Division in the early 1980s.

After 138 League appearances for Leicester, scoring eight goals between 1980 and 1984, MacDonald was signed by Joe Fagan in the hope that he would help to fill the midfield role vacated by the departure of Graeme Souness. Like Souness, MacDonald was strong in the tackle and could score and set up chances for his teammates. The trouble was that, apart from Bryan Robson, there were not really any comparable goalscoring world-class midfielders around in the mid-1980s good enough to fill Souness' boots. Anyone that Liverpool brought to Anfield during this period was bound to lose out when compared to Graeme Souness. John Wark had the same struggle on his hands.

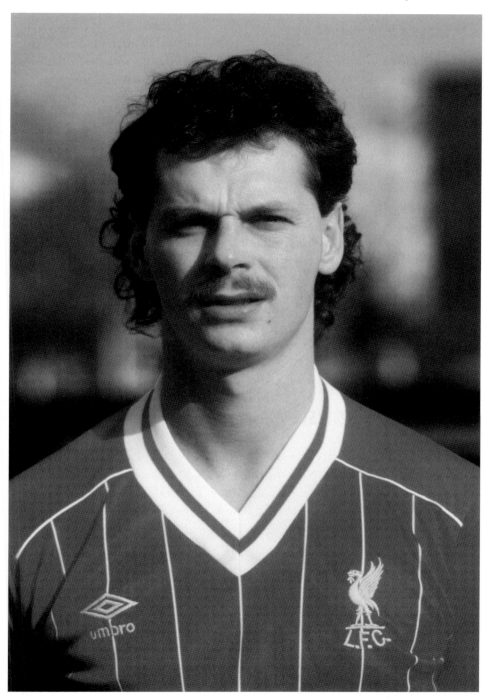

Kevin MacDonald

Joe Fagan handed MacDonald his first-team League debut against Luton Town in December 1984. John Wark scored Liverpool's goal in a 1-0 victory at Anfield. MacDonald had a run of 12 games in Fagan's team, but dropped out of contention towards the end of the season.

The 1985/86 campaign was a fabulous season for the Reds, winning the League and FA Cup double. MacDonald was in the Liverpool side that beat Everton in the FA Cup final. Although he had only started ten League games, his appearances as a substitute enabled him to collect a League Championship medal to go with his FA Cup one. A glittering future at Anfield looked to be there for the taking by MacDonald when tragedy struck. He suffered a badly broken leg playing against Southampton and that effectively ended his 1986/87 season.

When Kevin MacDonald did regain full fitness he never regained his place in the Liverpool side and had spells on loan back at Leicester and also with Glasgow Rangers who at the time had Graeme Souness as manager. After 56 League appearances for the Reds, MacDonald signed for Coventry City in July 1989.

Chapter 5

The idea of appointing Kenny Dalglish as Liverpool manager had actually been in the minds of the Anfield hierarchy well before the Heysel disaster. Joe Fagan was never going to enjoy a long reign at the helm at Liverpool, being sixty-two years of age when he took the job. The Liverpool directors obviously saw something in Kenny Dalglish that gave them confidence to believe that becoming player-manager at Anfield would not ask too much of the supremely talented Scot.

Everton, after romping to the First Division title and also winning the European Cup-Winners' Cup, looked set to rule the roost on Merseyside and in the English game in general for years to come. Dalglish knew that he was under severe pressure, 'I knew that quite a few people hoped that I would fall flat on my face and it gave me great pleasure to prove them wrong', Dalglish remarked after his first season in charge. 'I was desperate to succeed for the Liverpool supporters', he went on. 'I could never stand on the Kop, but I tried to please those who did. I would have loved to have joined them because I was a fan myself. I was just fortunate that I got a chance to follow the dream to become a professional footballer.'

When it came to his teammates at Anfield, the appointment of Dalglish as manager surprised some of them. Jan Molby remarked:

> I was surprised when Kenny was chosen. He didn't come across as someone who would like to be a manager. There are two completely different Kenny Dalglishes. The one where he didn't say much in interviews and the one he allowed the players to see. He has a great sense of humour. If Kenny trusted you he was fine.

Alan Hansen had been a teammate of Kenny Dalglish for many years at Anfield and was also a personal friend. Hansen said of his new boss, 'Kenny is such a football nut that you could mention any player in England and he'd know who you were talking about. He is his own man. He's also a moaning twit. He never leaves us alone on the pitch, but he's always been the same.'

Ian Rush, who had been on the receiving end of many a tongue-lashing from Dalglish over the years, said of the new Liverpool manager, 'Kenny was always giving advice and occasionally rollickings. He was full of encouragement and he helped to turn me into something more than just a goalscorer.'

Kenny Dalglish's style of management was to keep everyone on their toes, with selection for the Liverpool first team not a thing that anyone could take for granted. Mark Lawrenson was one of the best defenders in Europe during this period, but even he said that he was not certain of selection under Dalglish: 'Frankly you weren't quite sure when you won 5-0 whether you'd be playing the following week. With Bob Paisley, yes, with Joe Fagan, yes, with Kenny, no, not sure.'

Craig Johnston, like the rest of his Liverpool teammates knew what the new boss was up to with his trick of keeping everyone on their toes. Johnston revealed:

At Liverpool if there is ever any danger of over-confidence creeping into your game, or if you relax a fraction, you only have to look at the bench. There you will see someone who is good enough or hungry enough to take your place. No-one in this team ever lacks motivation.

Obviously it took Kenny Dalglish a little time to settle into his new role as player-manager at Anfield. The Reds won 6 of their first 11 League games, but Manchester United were the early pace setters with 10 wins in their first 10 games. As expected, Everton and, somewhat surprisingly, West Ham were also beginning to emerge as potential challengers for the title. As manager, Dalglish also had the problem of whether to select himself in the starting line-up. He was still an outstanding performer, but initially he used himself sparingly in the first team. He selected himself in only 8 of the first 22 League games and two of them were appearances from the substitutes' bench. One game that Dalglish did select himself for was the 3-2 victory over Everton at Goodison Park in the September 1985 derby match. After that it wasn't until the New Year that Dalglish played in the Reds first team on a more regular basis. Dalglish's absence from the team puzzled Liverpool fans and former boss Bob Paisley had little doubt at all that the Scot should have been selecting himself as often as possible. Paisley said, 'I know it's difficult, but Kenny should write down his own name first on the team sheet. Liverpool, with him playing, are a much better team. It's as simple as that.'

Paisley, along with most of the Liverpool boot room staff from the Shankly era, was still on hand at Anfield to help Dalglish through his early days at the

Kenny Dalgish celebrates with Ian Rush after Liverpool's 3-1 victory over Everton in the 1986 FA Cup final. Rush scored two and Craig Johnston the other one in Liverpool's victory.

helm. The new Liverpool boss once remarked, 'It was my first job as a manager and I had Bob Paisley, Tom Saunders, Roy Evans and Ronnie Moran standing right next to me, people I could trust. Without the help of the backroom staff I couldn't have continued playing.'

One player that Dalglish did select for the Reds' team on a regular basis was Jan Molby. Molby had been a revelation under Dalglish's management and in 39 League games knocked in 14 goals, an outstanding return for a midfield player. Molby admitted that under Joe Fagan he did not really display his best form. Molby recalled:

Joe Fagan brought me to Liverpool, but I found him frustrating. I played 22 games and then he left me out, just when I thought I was coming to terms with

The Liverpool squad record their FA Cup final song at a recording studio in Stockport in April 1986. Everyone at Anfield was singing after Dalglish's team completed the double with victory over Everton in the Wembley final.

English football. When Kenny took over, my career at Anfield took off. I got on very well with him and he was a big influence.

Jan Molby looked a different player under the new boss and within no time he also had quite a strong Scouse accent, something he put down to changing next to Sammy Lee.

With the prospect of competing in Europe out of the equation for the foreseeable future, Liverpool concentrated on winning as many of the domestic competitions as possible. After a good run in the League Cup, QPR knocked the Reds out of the competition 3-2 at the semi-final stage. In the two main domestic competitions, however, Liverpool were matching neighbours Everton stride for stride for League and FA Cup success. Liverpool took on Everton at Anfield in February 1986 in one of the most crucial derbies in recent years. Both teams were flying high at the top of the First Division and the winners were bound to be installed as the bookies' favourites for the title. Ron

Atkinson's Manchester United, along with West Ham, were also in the shake-up for the First Division crown, so victory was vital for both teams. Everton had the outstanding striker Gary Lineker in their line-up, but it was skipper Kevin Ratcliffe who struck the first blow for the Blues. A speculative shot from twenty-five yards out by Ratcliffe somehow managed to beat Bruce Grobbelaar in the Liverpool goal to give Everton a seventy-third minute lead. Twelve minutes from the end Gary Lineker then showed why he was regarded as the best English striker of his generation when he sealed victory for Everton with a superb lob over Grobbelaar to make it 2-0. At that moment in time Liverpool's title ambitions looked slim. Liverpool skipper, Alan Hansen, recalled his feelings after their derby disaster, 'I told Kenny after Everton turned us over 2-0 at Anfield that it was the worst side of individuals I had ever played in. A few weeks later I captained the team to the double. It just shows you how good my judgment was.'

Liverpool's shattering defeat against Everton gave Dalglish's team the kick up the backside that was needed to kick-start their faltering season. The Reds went on to win 11 of their final 12 League fixtures to win the title by two points from Everton, in second place, with West Ham four points behind Liverpool in third spot. Manchester United had been in the running until an end-of-season slump saw them fall away dramatically. United had actually won their first ten League games and at that early stage of the season Dalglish's side were ten points behind Ron Atkinson's team. West Ham, like Liverpool, ended the campaign in stunning form, including an 8-1 thrashing of Newcastle United. After narrowly failing to retain their title, Everton were determined to stop Kenny Dalglish's team completing the double in the 1986 FA Cup final.

Liverpool had had some close games on the road to Wembley, including a narrow 2-1 victory away at Watford in the quarter-finals. The first game at Anfield ended 0-0 and Liverpool travelled to Watford six days later expecting a stern test. Goals from Jan Molby and Ian Rush put Liverpool into the semi-finals, but it was a close call. Jan Molby admitted that the pressure was certainly on him when Liverpool were awarded a spot-kick. Liverpool were 1-0 down with just four minutes to play. He recalled:

I looked around me, the ball was in the penalty area waiting to be put on the spot and virtually the whole of my teammates were walking in the opposite direction. Kenny Dalglish, who was playing that day, just looked up at me and said 'You'. If I missed it, I would never be forgiven. I would be the one to blame for our Cup exit and the chance of the double would be gone.

Molby did convert the penalty kick to keep Liverpool in the FA Cup. Ian Rush then scored a dramatic winner in extra time to complete a memorable comeback for the Reds.

Liverpool played Southampton in the semi-finals of the FA Cup. The build-up to the semi-final game against Southampton, with Everton taking on Sheffield Wednesday in the other tie, was as intense as any couple of matches involving Merseyside's big two football clubs that had ever been witnessed. Liverpool and Everton had met at Wembley the previous season in the League Cup final, but this was the big one. In the 1980s the FA Cup was still regarded as the greatest domestic knockout cup competition in the world, bar none.

Southampton were determined to spoil the prospect of an all-Merseyside final and made confident noises before the game. 'We are capable of scoring against any team. It's a one-off game and we've got a score to settle after losing at home to Liverpool', said Southampton striker Danny Wallace before the game.

Southampton manager Chris Nicholl remarked, 'With goalkeepers of the quality of Grobbelaar and Shilton playing there won't be many goals. Liverpool as a team, however, are getting into their stride now. There's also the fact that Kenny Dalglish is back playing and he's in outstanding form at the moment.'

Chris Nicholl's prediction of few goals proved spot on and the first ninety minutes ended with the game all-square at 0-0. The game, which was played at White Hart Lane, then went into extra-time and Liverpool's goalscorer supreme, Ian Rush, struck twice to send his team into the 1986 FA Cup final. Everton overcame Sheffield Wednesday in the other semi-final to set up the first ever all-Merseyside FA Cup final in history.

PAUL WALSH

Paul Walsh was born in Plumstead, London. He began his career as an apprentice with Charlton Athletic in 1979. Charlton let him go to Luton Town in July 1982 for a £250,000 fee and he developed into an outstanding young striker. Bob Paisley offered Luton £700,000 for Walsh and he signed for the Reds in the summer of 1984.

Walsh made his debut against Norwich City at Carrow Road in the first match of the 1984/85 season. The game ended in a 3-3 draw. Walsh then scored in his Anfield debut, a 3-0 victory over West Ham. John Wark scored

Paul Walsh

the Reds' other goals. Paul Walsh scored two more in the opening weeks of the new season before the first of a number of injuries that would dog his Anfield career hit him. He was out of action until just before Christmas and didn't really hit goalscoring form until the final months of the campaign when he knocked in 5 goals in Liverpool's last 9 League games. He had scored 13 goals in League and cup games during his first season at Anfield, but had only played in half the First Division fixtures.

On the international stage, Paul Walsh had made his England debut while still at Luton Town, against Australia in June 1983. The game ended in a 0-0 draw. Walsh played a few days later, once again against Australia, and scored his only international goal in England's 1-0 victory. After five appearances Paul Walsh never represented England again. His international selection, similar to his Liverpool career, was never really helped by his lengthy lay-offs through injury.

Paul Walsh's best season at Anfield was Liverpool's title-winning campaign of 1985/86. Despite the fact that he only made 17 League appearances, he scored 11 valuable goals that were crucial in Liverpool's two-point title victory over neighbours Everton. West Ham finished four points behind the Reds in third spot.

Walsh had better luck with injuries during the 1986/87 campaign making 23 appearances and scoring 6 goals.

By the following season the attacking positions in the Liverpool side were mainly taken by Aldridge, Beardsley and Barnes and Paul Walsh decided to try his luck back in London after Spurs paid Liverpool £500,000 for his services.

MICHAEL ROBINSON

Leicester-born Michael Robinson began his football career playing in Blackpool Schoolboy teams. As a teenager he continued his football development playing for a Blackpool Sunday League side by the name of Dolphinstone Football Club. An offer then came his way to join Preston North End as an apprentice and he turned professional in July 1976.

Robinson impressed at Preston scoring 15 goals in 45 appearances. Manchester City made Preston a £756,000 offer for their young striker and he signed for Malcolm Allison's team in July 1979. Robinson's spell at Maine Road was not a success and he played just 29 times for City, scoring 8 goals. Brighton came in with a £400,000 offer to City for Robinson's services and he signed for them in July 1980.

Michael Robinson celebrates Liverpool's 1984 League Cup victory over Everton with Alan Hansen and Graeme Souness. Robinson is now a leading television football pundit in Spain.

Michael Robinson's career really took off at Brighton and he scored 37 goals in 111 appearances. Robinson was in the Brighton side that was defeated by Manchester United in the FA Cup final of 1983. Brighton held United to a draw in the first game, but lost the replay 4-0; Michael Robinson actually set up Gordon Smith with a carefully placed pass in the final seconds of the first game, but Smith fluffed his chance of bringing the FA Cup to Brighton for the first time.

Michael Robinson's form for Brighton caught the eye of Liverpool boss Joe Fagan and he joined the Reds for £200,000 in August 1983. Robinson made his Liverpool debut against Wolves at the start of the 1983/84 season. Ian Rush scored Liverpool's goal in a 1-1 draw.

Robinson's first goal for the Reds was away at West Ham in October 1983 and his stunning hat-trick gave Fagan's boys a 3-1 victory. It looked like Robinson was going to be a goalscoring sensation at Anfield, but throughout the rest of the campaign he only managed to find the net three more times.

His goal tally of 6 in 24 appearances looked rather paltry when compared to Ian Rush's 32 goals in 41 appearances.

Michael Robinson was, however, a whole-hearted performer in the red shirt of Liverpool and was rewarded with a League Championship medal in his first season at the club. He also picked up a European Cup winners' medal in the 1983/84 campaign, coming on as a substitute for Kenny Dalglish in the final against Roma which the Reds won on penalties after extra time.

Michael Robinson's brief spell at Anfield ended after just 51 appearances when he joined QPR in December 1984. The fee was £100,000. Robinson's Liverpool career yielded 13 goals in League and Cup games. He also won 23 caps for the Republic of Ireland between 1980 and 1986.

Robinson's career ended at Osasuna in the Spanish League and he began a new one commentating on La Liga for Spanish television.

Jim Beglin tackles Boniek of Juventus in the 1985 European Cup final. Juventus won the game 1-0 through a Platini penalty, but few cared as the tragic events that took place before the match rendered the result virtually meaningless.

JIM BEGLIN

Waterford-born Jim Beglin began his football career with Shamrock Rovers in the early 1980s. Liverpool's scouting network in Southern Ireland sent back glowing reports about the young Shamrock Rovers full-back and for a nominal fee, Beglin joined the Reds in May 1983.

Jim Beglin spent a season adjusting to life at Anfield and when his first-team chance did arrive it was not playing in his favoured full-back position, but in midfield against Southampton at Anfield. The November 1984 fixture ended in a disappointing 1-1 draw and Beglin did not feature in a League game for the Reds again until four months later when Joe Fagan selected him at left-back against Sunderland. The Reds won the away fixture 3-0 and Jim Beglin played at full-back for most of the remaining fixtures.

The 1985/86 season was the one in which Jim Beglin established himself in the Liverpool first team and he ended up as new manager Kenny Dalglish's first choice at left-back for most of the campaign. Beglin picked up his only honours during this momentous season at Anfield with FA Cup and League Championship medals.

At this stage in his career Jim Beglin was also an established member of the Republic of Ireland side and had played in a European Cup final, taking the injured Alan Kennedy's place against Juventus at Heysel Stadium in 1985. Similar in many ways to the unfortunate circumstances that conspired to end Kevin MacDonald's Anfield career, Jim Beglin also sustained a dreadful injury that wrecked what should have been a long and fruitful Liverpool career. Playing against Everton in a League Cup quarter-final tie early in 1987, Beglin came out of a tackle with Gary Stevens with a badly broken leg. It was an accident, but the damage was done.

After that, Jim Beglin's Liverpool career never got back on track and in June 1989 he signed for Leeds United on a free transfer. Jim Beglin also had spells at Plymouth and Blackburn, but at all three clubs he managed only 30 League appearances before having to retire from football. It was definitely a sad tale of what might have been when summing up Jim Beglin's Anfield career. He made 90 appearances for the Reds, scoring 3 goals.

Chapter 6

It seemed like the whole of Merseyside converged on London for the 1986 FA Cup final. Some reports claimed that tickets were changing hands for as much as £1,000.

Craig Johnston had enjoyed a fine season during Kenny Dalglish's first term as manager and told the *Daily Star* that the Scot was a tremendous boss. Johnston said:

> Last year for the first time in ten years Liverpool failed to win anything. This season with the same squad plus Steve McMahon we are going for the double. What's the difference? I'll tell you in two words, Kenny Dalglish. He is a manager who found something in me and in Jan Molby. Both our Liverpool careers were going nowhere last season. Since Kenny arrived we have now got a decent chance. The biggest thing about the boss is his honesty. If you put in 100 per cent for him you get your rewards. There's a new dimension to Liverpool, he's restored the old title-winning bounce to the side.

Liverpool's captain for the final against Everton, Alan Hansen, was determined to win the double. Hansen told the press:

> We have a saying at Liverpool, 'First is first and second is nowhere.' Some people are happy just to appear in an FA Cup final. I myself don't think that you can call it a great day if we lose. Only two captains in Liverpool's history, Ron Yeats and Emlyn Hughes have lifted the FA Cup. I want to become the third.

Liverpool's attempt to become only the third team in modern times to win the double began badly. Newly crowned 'Footballer of the Year' Gary Lineker gave the Blues the lead after eighteen minutes. Bruce Grobbelaar then had to make a fantastic save from Graeme Sharp to stop Everton going 2-0 up.

Liverpool were in disarray until Jan Molby began to display the outstanding form that had made him such a crowd favourite at Anfield in their title-winning campaign. Molby set up Ian Rush for Liverpool's equaliser after fifty-seven minutes. Then, six minutes later, Craig Johnston put the Reds into the lead from close range. Jan Molby was now running the game and it was no surprise to see him send Ronnie Whelan through with a pass from midfield. Whelan found Rush who shot past Bobby Mimms to clinch the FA Cup for Liverpool. In his first season as Liverpool boss Kenny Dalglish had achieved what no other Anfield manager had managed, the League and FA Cup double.

Many soccer pundits thought that if a team from Merseyside was going to achieve the double during the 1985/86 season then it would be the one from Goodison Park. Liverpool's FA Cup final star, Jan Molby, also admitted this after the Wembley final, 'We were so far behind Everton in the League that nobody thought that we could catch them. It was Everton who were favourites for the double, we just thought whatever we achieved would be great.'

Kenny Dalglish found time to congratulate Everton after the final when he said, 'Everton haven't done anything wrong, they finished second in the League

Action from the first ever all-Merseyside FA Cup final in 1986. Liverpool's Lawrenson, Nicol and Hansen fight for the ball with Lineker and Sheedy of Everton.

Liverpool's Kenny Dalglish outpaces Everton's Peter Reid and Paul Bracewell in the 1986 FA Cup final.

and runners-up in the Cup. Both Liverpool and Everton and their supporters are a credit to Merseyside'. Of the final itself Dalglish said:

I thought we played well in the first half and at half-time felt that all we had to do was keep going. When you've got Rushie playing like that, you've always got a chance of winning. I feel absolutely delighted. I'm just fortunate to work with the best group of players and backroom staff in Britain. I've got to pinch myself. Winning the double is a dream come true.

Liverpool captain Alan Hansen was thrilled to become only the third Reds captain to lift the FA Cup. Hansen told the press that he was determined to get up to the Royal Box ahead of Dalglish to lift the trophy:

Kenny got in ahead of me to collect the League Championship trophy, but there was no way he was going up the steps first today. He didn't even make one shot at goal today. When I get back to the dressing-room I'm going to tell him it's time for him to retire.

Kenny Dalglish, Jan Molby and Ronnie Whelan congratulate Ian Rush on his first goal against Everton in the 1986 FA Cup final. Rush scored twice in Liverpool's historic victory that won them the League and FA Cup double.

As for the final itself, Hansen said:

Everton got more tired than us. I thought they were going to bury us at the start of the second half, but we came back fighting. That's what Liverpool are all about. To be honest, we've not had much success at Liverpool, so we were due to win something eventually!

Members of the Everton camp, though dejected to have missed out on the double themselves after pushing Liverpool so close, found time to pay tribute to Kenny Dalglish and his team. Peter Reid remarked, 'A lot of people were saying afterwards that Jan Molby was their match winner. For me it was Ian Rush. Rushie was magnificent. People talk about world-class players and he ranks among them. He's a fabulous, fabulous footballer.'

Liverpool captain, Alan Hansen, holds the FA Cup aloft after his team had beaten Everton 3-1 in the 1986 FA Cup final.

The Liverpool team celebrate their fabulous victory over Everton.

Liverpool parade the FA Cup around Wembley after their victory.

Double winners Liverpool parade the League Championship and FA Cup through the streets of Liverpool.

Everton defender Derek Mountfield, talking about the Liverpool team of the 1980s remarked, 'In those days Liverpool were relentless. They would keep on going for the whole ninety minutes and grind teams down.'

Everton manager Howard Kendall paid tribute to Kenny Dalglish and his team when he said:

Winning the championship by scoring the vital goal himself against Chelsea was a magnificent achievement. Kenny has had his critics for not playing himself more often and for playing different systems with either a sweeper or an orthodox back four. Kenny was determined to do it his way. Although he had got 16 or 17 senior players, I have not heard one of them complain when he has been left out. They respect him that much. When he's out on the pitch he calms things down and sets an example with his determination and will to win. That rubs off on the other players.

The Liverpool team celebrated their tremendous achievement by spending the evening at Stringfellows club in London. Jan Molby recalled:

We made our way around to Stringfellows and showed the doorman the FA Cup. All the boys were there – Kenny, Alan Hansen – and I remember having my photograph taken with snooker star, Alex Higgins and the FA Cup. We then had a cramped journey on the flight back to Liverpool. We shared the same plane as the Everton team. I remember Pat Van den Hauwe saying to Sammy Lee, 'Move your fat arse!' Sammy said, 'Sorry, but what do you expect, I've got two bloody winners medals in my back pocket.'

Basking in the glory of winning the double in just his first season as player-manager at Anfield, Kenny Dalglish spent the summer months pondering on whether the time was now right to retire as a player. 'I've still got two years left on my contract as a player and I've certainly not decided to hang up my boots. Let's just say that I will play again next season if selected', declared the Liverpool boss.

Kenny Dalglish did play again during the 1986/87 campaign, making 18 League appearances for Liverpool, 6 of these from the bench. He still managed to score six goals in what turned out to be a disappointing campaign by Liverpool's standards. They finished second in the League, nine points behind Everton and runners-up in the Football League Cup. Arsenal beat Dalgish's team 2-1 in the final. Liverpool's attempts to retain the FA Cup also came to an early end, losing 3-0 in a second replay at Luton after the first two games ended 0-0.

With Kenny Dalglish at the helm, however, Liverpool were never going to become a club satisfied with second best and the following season they once again came close to achieving the FA Cup double.

STEVE MCMAHON

Steve McMahon began his professional football career at Goodison Park. He was even an Everton ball-boy as a youth and a long career in the blue shirt looked to be on the cards.

The Liverpool-born midfielder had broken into the Everton side by the time he was in his late teens. Then, out of the blue, McMahon declined the contract offer that Everton boss Howard Kendall put before him and he signed for Aston Villa in 1983.

Steve McMahon

Liverpool wanted to take him to Anfield as soon as they heard that Everton were about to sell him to Villa, but McMahon chose to start anew in the Midlands. McMahon had made 100 appearances for Everton and it was a bitter blow to Kendall that one of the best young midfielders in the country was no longer at Goodison. At Aston Villa, Steve McMahon continued to look a class act and Liverpool eventually got their man when Kenny Dalglish offered £350,000 for him in May 1983. McMahon had never really been happy in the Midlands and jumped at the chance to return to Merseyside.

At Anfield McMahon's career really blossomed and he played a key part in Liverpool's double winning season of 1985/86. His Reds debut was against Oxford United on 14 September 1985 – the game ended in a 2-2 draw. A week later McMahon was in the Liverpool side that travelled to Goodison and beat Everton 3-2, the former Blues ball-boy scoring a dramatic winner. McMahon, after his display at Goodison, was an instant hit with the Anfield faithful and by the time he left Liverpool in 1991 he had also collected three League Championship medals to go with his FA Cup one.

In 1988 Steve McMahon's fine form for Liverpool brought him to the attention of the England manager and he made his international debut in a 0-0 draw with Israel in Tel Aviv in February of that year. McMahon went on to win 17 England caps during his days at Anfield.

By the time Steve McMahon signed for Manchester City, for a £900,000 fee in December 1991, he had made 264 appearances for Liverpool, scoring 49 goals. McMahon made 87 appearances for City before joining Swindon Town in 1994. He then went on to manage Swindon after his playing days drew to a close

GARY ABLETT

Liverpool-born Gary Ablett was one of that select band of players who represented both Everton and Liverpool in a fine professional career.

After serving his football apprenticeship at Liverpool, Kenny Dalglish handed Gary Ablett his Football League debut against Charlton on 20 December 1986. The game ended in a 0-0 draw.

The versatile defender went on to make four more League appearances for the Reds during that season. In one of those games Gary Ablett managed to score the only League goal of his Anfield career in Liverpool's 3-0 victory over Nottingham Forest. Although Liverpool finished the campaign trophyless, Gary Ablett had forced his way into Dalglish's squad.

Gary Ablett in action against Everton's Adrian Heath – Ablett is the only player to have won the FA Cup with both Everton and Liverpool.

Over the next few seasons Gary Ablett was a first-team player at Anfield on a more regular basis. Ablett could play at either full-back or in the centre of defence and picked up his first silverware for the Reds when they won the League title in 1988. He played in 17 of Liverpool's League games.

The following season saw Ablett become a regular first-team choice, playing in 35 of Liverpool's League games. He was also in the Liverpool side that defeated Everton 3–2 in the all-Merseyside FA Cup final of 1989. At the time it was thought that Gary Ablett would now be a virtual ever-present in the Reds defence, but the 1989/90 season saw him playing second fiddle again to Hansen and Hysen at the centre of the Liverpool defence. He came into the side to cover for injuries and only appeared in 15 League games throughout the campaign. At the end of the 1989/90 season Liverpool were once again title winners and Gary Ablett picked up his second championship medal.

Throughout his career at Anfield, Gary Ablett had always been a much sought after player from other top clubs who were prepared to give the talented defender regular first-team football. When Everton offered new Liverpool boss Graeme Souness £750,000 for Ablett in January 1992, Liverpool decided to part with him.

Gary Ablett had made 144 appearances in the red of Liverpool. During his career at Anfield he also had spells on loan at Derby County and Hull City.

Chapter 7

If season 1986/87 was an unhappy one for Liverpool when it came to their pursuit of silverware, there was also the loss of Ian Rush to Juventus to contend with. The Rush deal had been set up in June 1986, but it still came as a bitter blow when Liverpool fans gathered at Anfield for the 4 May 1986 fixture against Watford. As expected, Ian Rush scored in his farewell game for the Reds, but it was hard to believe that this would be the last they would see of one of the greatest strikers in Liverpool's history. Rush's tally of 30 goals in 42 appearances during his farewell season displayed once again that as a striker he had few equals in European football.

Kenny Dalglish, with the imminent departure of Rush in mind, paid Oxford United £700,000 for John Aldridge in January 1987. Aldridge turned out to be a fantastic striker for Dalglish's team with 61 goals in 88 appearances. In an all-out attempt to recapture the League title from Everton, Kenny Dalglish also made big-money purchases in John Barnes, Peter Beardsley and Ray Houghton. All would turn out to be fantastic acquisitions to the Liverpool team, with Barnes destined to achieve legendary status by the time his Anfield career had drawn to a close.

Barnes and Beardsley made their League debuts for Liverpool in the opening game of the season against Arsenal at Highbury. Goals from Aldridge and Nicol gave the Reds a great start to the new campaign. Peter Beardsley had to leave the field of play after being on the receiving end of a bad tackle from Arsenal's Steve Williams. Beardsley later remarked, 'He put his studs down my leg. I felt Steve had done me deliberately. I got another knock in the game later on and had to limp off.'

The Liverpool teams of this era also had their fair share of tough characters, none more so than Steve McMahon, and former Liverpool boss Bob Paisley said of the tenacious midfielder, 'When Steve McMahon plays well, Liverpool play well. He is tough and indomitable.'

Alan Hansen is applauded by his teammates as he walks on to the pitch at Anfield to accept the 1988 League Championship trophy. Hansen won eight League titles during his Liverpool career.

Since taking over as manager, Kenny Dalglish had had the guidance and inspiration of the likes of Bob Paisley and Ronnie Moran when he needed experienced advice. Liverpool might have won the League and FA Cup double in his first year as manager, but at Anfield, basking in the glory of trophy wins did not last long. Preparing for future success was the key to continued dominance of the English game and Ronnie Moran, who had been at Anfield even before Shankly arrived at the club in 1959, said the future was all that mattered:

> We were always brought up on the theory that if you won or lost in a game, you carried on the same. It worked. You didn't let players go too high in the sky because you wanted them level-headed ready for the next game. If you lost a game at Liverpool you overcame it quickly ready for the next game.

Although Liverpool under Dalglish had proved themselves to be the kings of the English game, not being able to compete against the best in Europe was still hard to come to terms with for a club of Liverpool's standing in the game. Ronnie Moran said of Liverpool's European ban after Heysel:

It was a bad thing for English football. Even in the early days of Liverpool competing in Europe it was a lot different than playing in a League or even an international game. In Europe you played against club sides who were very well organized. Even against the so called lesser teams in Europe, they would still give you a hard time.

Liverpool's outstanding team of the mid to late 1980s was destined never to compete against Europe's finest. By the time Christmas 1987 arrived Dalglish's team had still to taste defeat in the League. Everton had knocked the Reds out of the League Cup with a 1-0 win at Anfield in October, but in the First Division Liverpool were untouchable. John Aldridge was enjoying a sensational season and the absence of Ian Rush was hardly noticed. John Aldridge's double

Alan Hansen presents the Liverpool team to Princess Diana before the 1988 FA Cup final. Liverpool lost the game 1-0 to Wimbledon.

against Newcastle at Anfield on Boxing Day took his League tally for the season to 17 goals.

John Barnes was also enjoying a fantastic first season at Anfield. Former Liverpool full-back Alan Kennedy was as impressed as everyone else was at Anfield. When asked about Barnes Kennedy said, 'He needed somebody to show faith in him. That is exactly what Kenny has done. John Barnes works hard and floats around the pitch causing opposition defenders all manner of problems. Only now is he being fully appreciated.'

Dalglish himself said that from the very first moment he arrived at Anfield John Barnes had looked outstanding: 'He was a magnificent player who worked harder than anyone could imagine. His class was obvious from his first training session at Melwood.'

The 1987/88 campaign appeared to be a season when every member of the Liverpool team seemed to hit peak form. John Barnes himself said that the most underrated player at Anfield was Steve Nicol. 'Stevie Nicol was our secret weapon. He often played a major role in games without getting the headlines,' declared Barnes.

John Aldridge said that by the time 1988 had arrived the feeling inside Anfield was that the First Division title was already in the bag. Aldridge declared:

By the turn of the year there was little doubt that Liverpool would win the League. In John Barnes and Peter Beardsley we had two of the best players in the country. Steve McMahon was orchestrating things superbly in midfield. In defence we had the class of Hansen and Gillespie, Venison and Ablett. In midfield we had Houghton, Whelan and Spackman. You could see why we won 22 and drew 6 of our opening 28 League games.

By the time March 1988 had arrived Liverpool were still unbeaten in the League. The next opponents for Dalglish's team were city neighbours Everton. Liverpool needed to avoid defeat in the game to beat Leeds United's 1973/74 record of 29 games unbeaten. Everton might have been trailing Liverpool by a wide margin in the table, but a goal by Wayne Clarke gave the blue half of Merseyside some reason to be cheerful on that Sunday afternoon back in March 1988. It was the only goal of the game and Liverpool's sensational unbeaten run had finally come to an end. Liverpool, as expected, went on to win the title by a big points margin, with Manchester United nine points behind the Reds in second spot. Nottingham Forest, managed by Brian Clough, finished third. Liverpool's sensational 5-0 slaughter of Clough's team in April 1988 is a game still talked about to this day. Football legend Sir Tom Finney attended the game and after it remarked, 'Liverpool must be the best team of all time. It was the finest exhibition of football that I have seen during all my time playing and watching the game.'

Kenny Dalglish recently said of the Nottingham Forest game:

I've got a video of that match. I still get excited simply getting it out of the box. Some of the football was magnificent. Even I didn't know what they were going to do and I was the man who picked the team and sent them out onto the pitch. It was a very exciting team.

Once again Kenny Dalglish was in charge of a side that had an outstanding chance to win the League and FA Cup double in just his third season in charge. After victories over Stoke, Aston Villa, Everton, Manchester City and Nottingham Forest the Reds faced Wimbledon in the 1988 FA Cup final. Liverpool were expected to accomplish their second double in three seasons with a comprehensive victory over Wimbledon. In the biggest FA Cup upset in years, the side that had been playing in the Southern League just eleven years prior to the 1988 final beat Dalglish's star-studded team 1-0. Wimbledon goalkeeper Dave Beasant played the game of his life, including stopping an Aldridge penalty kick and the football world was stunned. There was no real excuse from Liverpool who had been beaten by a team that simply looked more hungry for success on the day.

The 1987/88 season had been one of the most exhilarating in Anfield history. Many Liverpool regulars claim that the football on offer was the best ever seen in the club's history. Unbelievably, Dalglish's team would once again come incredibly close to achieving the League and FA Cup double a year later. The Hillsborough tragedy would, however, make Liverpool's football achievements seem of little significance.

JOHN ALDRIDGE

Liverpool-born striker John Aldridge began his football career at South Liverpool. He signed for Newport County in April 1979 and made 170 appearances for the Welsh side between 1979 and 1983. Aldridge's goal tally at Newport was 69. Oxford United signed Aldridge in March 1984 for a £78,000 fee.

John Aldridge is mobbed by ecstatic Liverpool fans after his team had just beaten Nottingham Forest in the 1988 FA Cup semi-final. Aldridge scored both goals in the 2-0 victory.

Aldridge's goalscoring prowess really blossomed at the Manor Ground and he netted 72 goals in 114 appearances. All the top clubs took a look at him, but it was Kenny Dalglish who took the plunge and paid Oxford £700,000 for Aldridge's services in January 1987. Ironically, the Reds could have signed Aldridge for nothing when he had trials at Anfield as a fourteen-year-old, but he was allowed to escape the net.

It was a dream come true for the boyhood Red when John Aldridge ran out at Villa Park in the red shirt of Liverpool to replace Paul Walsh for his League debut on 28 February 1987. Craig Johnston and Paul Walsh scored Liverpool's goals in a 2-2 draw. Aldridge opened his goalscoring account for the Reds against Southampton at Anfield the following week. After that he knocked in the goals for Liverpool on a regular basis. In 103 appearances between 1987 and 1989 he scored 61 goals.

Aldridge had predominantly been brought to Anfield to replace the departing Ian Rush who signed for Juventus at the end of the 1986/87 season. In his first season at Anfield Liverpool finished as runners-up in the League, but the following year they were champions. Aldridge scored 26 goals in 36 League appearances. John Aldridge could have capped his first full season at Anfield by being part of an FA Cup and First Division double-winning team, but unexpectedly Wimbledon beat the Reds 1-0 in the Wembley final in 1988.

John Aldridge's brief Liverpool career came to an end in 1989. The arrival of Ian Rush back at Anfield hastened Aldridge's departure from the club. Aldridge was a class act as a goalscorer, but Rush was certain to be given preference over him when it came to the main striker's role in the team. They had played together with a lot of success during the 1988/89 campaign and they even scored the three goals that defeated Everton 3-2 in the 1989 FA Cup final. Dalglish however made it clear that Ian Rush and John Barnes were his preferred choice in attack and Aldridge signed for Spanish club Real Sociedad for a £1 million transfer fee in September 1989.

John Aldridge's goalscoring exploits on Merseyside were, however, far from over and he scored a remarkable 115 goals for Tranmere Rovers in 185 appearances for the Birkenhead club between the years 1991 and 1996. For just £250,000 Tranmere secured the services of one of the most consistent goalscorers in English football history. John Aldridge made his mark on the international scene as well, making 68 appearances for the Republic of Ireland between 1986 and 1991.

NIGEL SPACKMAN

Nigel Spackman was born in Romsey, Hampshire. His football career began at Andover Town and Bournemouth signed the hard-working midfield player in May 1980. After 119 games for Bournemouth between 1980 and 1982 Spackman joined Chelsea for a £40,000 fee in 1983.

Nigel Spackman enjoyed a successful three years at Stamford Bridge, including helping them to win the Second Division title in 1984. He made 141 appearances in the blue of Chelsea before Kenny Dalglish made them a £400,000 offer for Spackman in February 1987. Dalglish got his man and gave Spackman his League debut against Southampton at Anfield on 28 February 1987. Ian Rush scored Liverpool's goal in a 1-0 victory.

Nigel Spackman played in most of Liverpool's games throughout the rest of the 1986/87 season. Liverpool missed out on the League title to Everton, but Spackman picked up his only Liverpool silverware the following season.

Nigel Spackman

Nigel Spackman had looked an impressive recruit to the Liverpool squad in his first few months at the club, but the fight for a regular first-team slot was something of a battle at Anfield during Dalglish's era as manager. Ronnie Whelan, Craig Johnston, Steve McMahon, Ray Houghton, Jan Molby and John Wark were all vying for a midfield place and Spackman did not get another lengthy run in the team until he was selected for the Boxing Day 1987 fixture at Oxford. Liverpool won 3-0 and Spackman retained his place in Dalglish's team until the end of the season. He played in 27 League games, 8 of them after coming on from the substitutes' bench.

After Liverpool's glorious title-winning campaign of the 1987/88 season, it looked like Nigel Spackman was in the first-team frame at Anfield for the foreseeable future. The following season, however, Spackman was selected to start in just eight League fixtures. He was also called on as a substitute four times.

After just 63 appearances for the Reds, Nigel Spackman left to join QPR for £500,000 in February 1989. He later spent time at Glasgow Rangers before returning to Stamford Bridge to finish his playing career at Chelsea.

PETER BEARDSLEY

Peter Beardsley's career began at Carlisle United in 1979. The Cumbrian club signed Beardsley from Wallsend Boys Club and he made 104 appearances for

Carlisle, scoring 22 goals. Beardsley then had a spell playing for Canadian side Vancouver Whitecaps who signed him from Carlisle in 1981 for £27,500.

Manchester United were then tipped off about the talented Longbenton-born youngster who was plying his trade in the Canadian League. They signed him for £150,000 in September 1982, but apart from playing in a few friendlies, he never made a first-team appearance at Old Trafford.

Beardsley returned to Vancouver Whitecaps the following year, before Newcastle offered them £120,000 to bring him back to England in September 1983. His career really took off at Newcastle and in 147 appearances he knocked in 61 goals.

Kenny Dalglish was determined to bring Beardsley to Anfield and even broke the British transfer record to secure his services. In the summer of 1987 Dalglish paid £1.9 million for Beardsley and along with another exciting new

Peter Beardsley

signing, John Barnes, he made his debut against Arsenal at the start of the 1987/88 season.

Beardsley took a little time to settle at Anfield, but when he did, the Liverpool fans could see that his massive transfer fee was money well spent. In his first season at the club Liverpool won the championship, Beardsley scoring 15 goals in 38 appearances. Peter Beardsley was also, at this stage in his career, an England regular having made his international debut against Egypt in Cairo in 1986. The partnership that he formed up front in the England side with Gary Lineker was quite exceptional and with a bit of luck could easily have led to World Cup success in the Mexico 1986 finals of the tournament.

Peter Beardsley had further success at Liverpool, playing his part in the Reds' 1989/90 League Championship victory and also their FA Cup triumph against Everton a year earlier. By the time Beardsley signed for Everton in 1991 for £1 million he had made 170 appearances for Liverpool, scoring 58 goals. For England Peter Beardsley made 59 appearances, scoring 9 goals but creating many more for his partner in attack, Gary Lineker.

Beardsley's career at Liverpool was not a long one, but his fabulous skills brought a great deal of pleasure to the Anfield faithful.

JOHN BARNES

John Barnes was one of the greatest players to wear the red shirt of Liverpool. Born in Kingston, Jamaica, Barnes began his football career playing for Sudbury Court. Watford signed the talented forward on a free transfer from the non-League club in July 1981 and turned him into one of the most talented and skilful players that the British game has ever seen. Barnes appeared in the 1984 FA Cup final for Watford against Everton and starred for them during the 1982/83 campaign when they finished runners-up in the First Division to Liverpool.

As soon as John Barnes became available for transfer, every leading club in the country fancied him, but it was Kenny Dalglish who secured his services for Liverpool in July 1987.

John Barnes had a fabulous first season at Anfield, the Reds winning the championship at a canter from Manchester United in second spot. Barnes' dazzling skills brought back memories of Peter Thompson and Steve Heighway at their best. Barnes' goal return of 15 in 38 League games was also quite phenomenal for a player who predominantly set up chances for the

John Barnes

likes of John Aldridge and, in later seasons, Ian Rush when he returned from Italy.

Barnes made his League debut for Liverpool at Highbury against Arsenal and goals from Aldridge and Nicol gave the Reds a flying start to the 1987/88 campaign with a 2-1 victory. Barnes' impressive form at Anfield led to him being voted the Player of the Year by both the PFA and the Football Writers' Association at the end of the 1987/88 season.

On the international stage, John Barnes was something of a disappointment for such a talented player. His fantastic goal against Brazil in Rio in 1984 looked to have heralded the arrival on the world scene of a global superstar. England won that game 2-0, Mark Hateley scoring the other goal. For England, however, John Barnes never really produced the breathtaking performances that became a regular occurrence in the red shirt of Liverpool.

Barnes won 79 caps for England, scoring 11 goals. After Barnes' wonderful first year at Anfield it came as something of a surprise to find his side losing out to Arsenal in the race for the First Division title. In the FA Cup, however, Barnes enjoyed being part of the team that beat Everton 3-2 in the final at Wembley.

The following season saw Barnes pick up his second championship medal at Anfield. He also won a League Cup winners' medal in 1995 which meant that he had achieved, at Liverpool, every domestic honour.

John Barnes ended a magnificent career with Liverpool when he signed for Newcastle on a free transfer in 1997. He later joined Charlton Athletic. He made 357 appearances for the Reds, scoring 101 goals. The £900,000 that Dalglish paid for him in 1987 was a sound piece of business.

RONNIE WHELAN

Ronnie Whelan was current Liverpool hero Steven Gerrard's favourite player when he watched the Reds as a youngster in the late 1980s and early 1990s. It is easy to see why Gerrard was influenced by Whelan. The Dublin-born midfielder was an inspirational figure in the great Liverpool sides of the 1980s. Just like Steven Gerrard, Whelan was always likely to pop up with a crucial goal when his team needed one the most. It was Ronnie Whelan who equalised against Spurs in the 1982 Football League Cup final with just minutes remaining. In the first period of extra time Whelan then put the Reds into the lead as Liverpool romped to a 3-1 victory. The following season saw Ronnie Whelan once again hitting the headlines in the 1983 Football League Cup final with a spectacular winner in Liverpool's 2-1 victory over Manchester United.

Ronnie Whelan

Ronnie Whelan came from a footballing family in Dublin. His father, Ronnie Whelan senior, played for St Patrick's Athletic and Drogheda and was also a full international for Eire.

Ronnie Whelan junior played for Home Farm, a Dublin feeder club for English sides such as Manchester United, Everton and Liverpool. Whelan spent brief periods training at Manchester United as a schoolboy, but it was Liverpool who gave him the opportunity to become a full-time professional in 1979.

Whelan made his debut for the Reds in April 1981. He scored in Liverpool's 3-0 victory against Stoke City, but did not become a first-team regular until the following season.

Ronnie Whelan made his full international debut for the Republic of Ireland in 1981 and went on to win 53 caps. His breakthrough season at Anfield was in 1981/82 when he made 32 League appearances, scoring 10 goals.

In the 1981/82 season, Ronnie Whelan was voted Young Player of the Year to add to the League Championship and League Cup medals that he also collected in an outstanding campaign for the young Dubliner. It was hard to believe that this was the same youngster who was so homesick in his early days at Anfield that his father virtually had to beg him to remain at Liverpool and not jump on the next boat back home to Dublin.

By the time Ronnie Whelan left Anfield for Southend United in September 1994, he had been a key member of the Liverpool side that had won twelve major trophies.

RAY HOUGHTON

Ray Houghton was born in Glasgow, but played international football for Eire. His first professional club was West Ham United, but after just one substitute appearance for the Hammers, he was allowed to join their London neighbours, Fulham, in July 1982. No transfer fee was involved and Fulham proved to be a good move for Houghton who made 129 appearances at Craven Cottage before moving to Oxford United.

Oxford paid £147,000 for the midfielder and Ray Houghton became a key figure in their 1986 Football League Cup triumph. Houghton's impressive midfield performances for Oxford soon came to the attention of new Republic of Ireland boss Jack Charlton. Through parentage, Houghton could be selected for Eire and Charlton awarded Houghton the first of 66 caps in 1986.

Ray Houghton displayed terrific form on the international stage and Kenny Dalglish paid Oxford £825,000 for the stocky midfielder in October 1987.

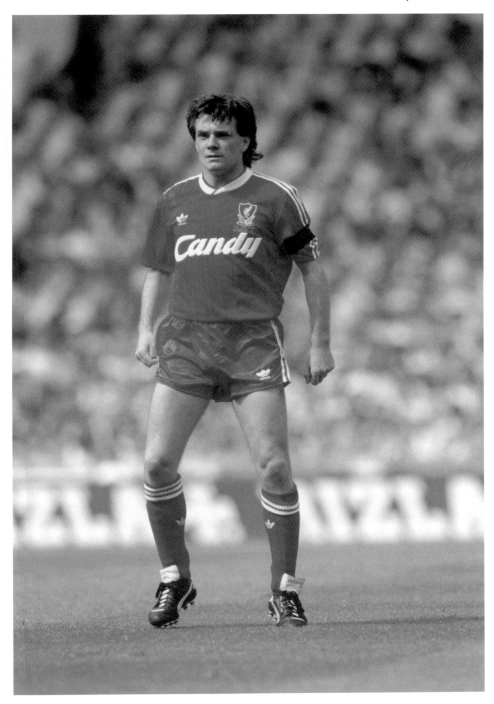

Ray Houghton

Ray Houghton's League debut for Liverpool came against Luton Town on the 24 October 1987. Gary Gillespie scored Liverpool's goal in a 1-0 victory.

Houghton more or less kept his place in the Reds' line-up for the remainder of the 1987/88 season and he looked an outstanding addition to Dalglish's team. The fact that the Eire international was also quite likely to score important goals for the Reds, although he was deployed wide on the right, all added to his importance to the team.

The 1989/90 season saw Ray Houghton's Liverpool appearances restricted by injury problems, but he still managed to play a role in the Reds' title-winning campaign.

Ray Houghton left Liverpool for Aston Villa in 1992 for a £825,000 transfer fee. He had won two League titles and two FA Cups during his Anfield career. Houghton made 95 appearances at Villa Park before Crystal Palace signed him for £300,000 in 1995.

Chapter 8

Kenny Dalglish prepared for the 1988/89 campaign with the added bonus that Ian Rush, after his unhappy season in the colours of Juventus, was back at Anfield. After the exhilarating football that Liverpool had displayed during the previous season, some questioned the wisdom of bringing Rush back to the club. John Aldridge had been a revelation when it came to finding the back of the net and new boys Beardsley and Barnes were straight out of the top drawer. Ian Rush was, however, a class act and once Dalglish knew that the goalscoring genius was available there was only one English club that Rush would be wearing the colours of in the coming season.

As it turned out, Ian Rush's first season back at Anfield was not the roaring success that many envisaged. He was selected for less than half of Liverpool's fixtures in the League making 16 appearances in Dalglish's side and another 8 from the substitutes' bench. Through a mixture of ill health and finding his feet again in the English game after his Italian disaster, it was not until the 1989/90 campaign that Rush looked to be back to his sharpest form.

In contrast, John Aldridge once again enjoyed a fine season, knocking in 21 goals in 35 League appearances, four of them from the bench. With Ian Rush's return to Anfield in mind, Aldridge knew that his days in the Liverpool first team might be numbered. In later years Aldridge spoke about his feelings when he found out that Rush was returning to the club:

> With hindsight I feel that I was brought in just to fill a gap until Ian Rush returned. I wasn't very happy. To score 63 goals in 104 games for Liverpool speaks for itself. At the end of the season I told Kenny I didn't want to leave Liverpool. He told me he wanted to form a partnership with Rushie and Peter Beardsley. All I wanted was a fair crack of the whip.

By February 1989 it looked like Arsenal would run away with the First Division title. They had built up a 19-point gap at the top of the League and Liverpool, who had lost 5 of their opening 19 games, were struggling. Everton's great 1980s revival was now in serious decline and it was only through a fantastic upsurge in form, from January until the end of the season, that Dalglish's team caught up with Arsenal at the top of the table.

Former Liverpool boss Bob Paisley rattled a few cages when he declared that the First Division was of the poorest quality that he had seen in years. Many disagreed with Paisley, but the Glasgow Rangers and England defender Gary Stevens agreed with the Anfield legend. Stevens said, 'I agree with Bob Paisley's statement that the current First Division is the worst he's seen. There are only a handful of teams capable of winning the League and Bob is right when he says that Liverpool are a cut above the rest.'

After Liverpool lost to Manchester United on New Year's Day 1989, it looked like the Reds' title defence had come to an early end. Liverpool then won 15 of their next 18 League matches and the battle for the 1988/89 League Championship came down to the final game of the season. It was Liverpool against Arsenal at Anfield on the 26 May for the greatest prize in English football. In a pulsating end-of-season clash the two teams went in at half-time with the score at 0-0. Arsenal needed to win the game by two clear goals to pip Liverpool for the title. Early in the second half Arsenal made the breakthrough when Alan Smith headed home a Winterburn free-kick. George Graham's team still needed one more goal and, with the ninety minutes of play nearly up, Lee Dixon sent a long ball to Smith who lobbed a speculative pass to Arsenal midfielder Michael Thomas. Thomas kept his cool and, after brushing off two Liverpool challengers, cleverly beat the onrushing Grobbelaar with a superbly judged flick into the net. The Liverpool fans inside Anfield were left stunned. The contingent of Arsenal fans who had made the journey to Merseyside went berserk. In the final moments of a pulsating game, their team had won the first League title since 1971. After they had got over the shock of what they had just witnessed Anfield rose as one to applaud the Arsenal team off the pitch. It had been one of the most dramatic nights in Anfield's history.

The events at Anfield on that warm early summer's evening in May 1989 were really of secondary importance to the tragedy that struck Liverpool Football Club a month prior to the end-of-season encounter with Arsenal. After victories over Carlisle, Millwall, Hull and Brentford, Liverpool took on Nottingham Forest in the semi-finals of the FA Cup. The venue was Hillsborough, the home of Sheffield Wednesday. At around 2.30p.m. on the afternoon of the 15 April 1989 Liverpool fans were streaming into the

Leppings Lane End of the ground. By 2.50p.m. a surge of fans, desperate to get into the ground in time for the 3.00p.m. kick-off, led to a crush. Noticing the dangerous situation that appeared to be worsening by the second, the police made a decision to open a large metal gate. Fans then surged in through this gate and crushed Liverpool fans already in the ground. Unaware that people at the front were badly injured, and in many instances dying, fans still continued to press forward. With the terrace in front of the Leppings Lane end of the ground being fenced in, there was no escape for the suffocating spectators.

A total of ninety-six Liverpool fans died as a result of the Hillsborough tragedy. Merseyside, like the whole of the country, was in a state of shock. Liverpool players from past and present could not believe what they had just witnessed. Former Reds' star, David Fairclough, who was playing in Belgium at the time, said he found out about what was happening at Hillsborough, as did millions more at home in Britain, while watching BBC television. Fairclough recalled:

We could pick up Grandstand in Belgium. I couldn't believe what was happening. I watched all the different channels to find out what was going on. In Belgium there was a negative response at first, but when everything unfolded the feeling turned to one of great sympathy.

Ray Houghton was in the Liverpool side for the semi-final tie and recalled when he first became aware of the Hillsborough tragedy unfolding:

In those first six minutes of play I can honestly say that not one player on the pitch or the referee realised that there were major problems. Then a lad dressed in Liverpool colours came on to the pitch and shouted to me, 'Ray, they are dying in there.' The referee then immediately led us off and back to the dressing rooms. The dressing room door was left open. I can't remember who said it, but the comment brought a stunned silence, 'I think Liverpool Football Club have got another Heysel on their hands.'

For weeks after the Hillsborough tragedy Liverpool Football Club, as well as the footballers and their wives and families, did what they could to help. Merseyside football was united in their grief. Everton did what they could to help, along with the team from across the Mersey, Tranmere Rovers. Anfield became a shrine with club colours and messages of sympathy from across the globe adorning the whole of the Kop terrace.

A decision was made for the FA Cup semi-final against Nottingham Forest to be rearranged and Old Trafford was chosen as the venue. Many wanted the

FA Cup to be abandoned for that season as a mark of respect to those that had died. Liverpool defeated Forest 3-1 in the rearranged game and met Everton in the 1989 FA Cup final. Generally an all–Merseyside FA Cup final would have been the source of great excitement between Blues and Reds fans before the match took place. The players themselves knew that they had to carry on in a professional manner, but some, like John Aldridge, said that for a time they didn't really have the heart for the game. 'There was a time when I wondered if I would ever master the strength to play. I seriously considered retirement', Aldridge said in his autobiography.

Liverpool defeated Everton 3-2 in the 1989 FA Cup final after extra time. After the events at Hillsborough, even fanatical Evertonians were not too bothered about the result. The game itself was as fiercely fought as any derby game had been, past or present, but most football supporters throughout the land were happy to see the FA Cup return to Anfield. Everton winger Pat Nevin said that the people of Liverpool's reaction to Hillsborough really touched him, 'Quite simply, that city couldn't have acted better in a more honourable way, a more thoughtful way than they did.'

Everton boss, Colin Harvey, said that both sides did the city proud. 'The game was very competitive, what we both wanted was a game that was played in the right spirit and the crowd to watch it in the right spirit, which they did.'

Kenny Dalglish regarded Liverpool's 1989 FA Cup win as special, 'The victory over Everton in 1989 was special because of the circumstances surrounding it. It was probably the victory that gave me the most satisfaction because it meant an awful lot to an awful lot of people. That one sticks in my mind.'

Liverpool's 3-2 victory after extra time came courtesy of two goals from Ian Rush, with John Aldridge scoring the other. Everton's two goals came from midfielder Stuart McCall. After the game the celebrations were very low key for Dalglish's team. Ray Houghton said that the Reds' victory after an emotional Wembley occasion caused little elation in the Liverpool camp, 'We had won it for Liverpool and their fans. There was no big celebration for the players. We went for a quiet meal in a hotel close to Leicester Square and then we went home.'

It was somehow fitting that after such a poignant victory it was the inspirational Ronnie Whelan who had the honour of receiving the FA Cup after taking over the Liverpool captaincy from the injured Alan Hansen.

The following season, 1989/90, in the aftermath of Hillsborough, was a difficult and trying one for all at Anfield. The fact that Kenny Dalglish managed to lead his team to the First Division title speaks volumes for the

Everton goalkeeper Neville Southall saves a goal-bound Liverpool attempt during the 1989 FA Cup final watched by John Aldridge. Liverpool won the final 3-2 after extra time.

resilience of the Liverpool boss and his team. During the course of Liverpool's last title-winning season in their history there were some spectacular victories, most notably the 9-0 demolition of Crystal Palace in September 1989, in John Aldridge's last game for the Reds before moving to Real Sociedad for a £1 million fee. Dalglish's team also hit Chelsea for five at Stamford Bridge just before Christmas and Coventry for six in the final game of the season in an away game at Highfield Road.

Liverpool's closest challengers were Graham Taylor's Aston Villa side. Villa ended the season a creditable nine points behind Liverpool, their highest League position since they had won the title in 1981.

Liverpool's FA Cup campaign in the 1989/90 season came to an unexpected end against the side that they had struck nine goals past earlier in the season. Every soccer pundit in the land expected Liverpool to see off Palace in the 1990 FA Cup semi-final game at Villa Park, but in an unbelievable encounter Crystal Palace put the Reds out 4-3 after extra time, Rush, McMahon and Barnes scoring the Liverpool goals.

To have won the League, however, was nothing short of a minor miracle, after the trauma of Hillsborough. Only those very close to Kenny Dalglish at the time really knew just how much all the tragedy had taken out of the Liverpool manager. The 1980s had been a golden decade for Liverpool and

Liverpool manager Kenny Dalglish holds the 1990 League Championship trophy. It was destined to be his final piece of silverware before he resigned as manager a year later.

their supporters when it came to winning football's glittering prizes. Few fans could have envisaged that Anfield would not witness a title-winning side playing in the red of Liverpool for the rest of the century and beyond. Liverpool's magnificent European Cup victory of 2005 moved the team from Anfield back into the big league of European football once again. There is also now a feeling of optimism that the days when Liverpool once ruled the English game, as they undoubtedly did for most of the 1980s, is no longer an unattainable dream.

IAN RUSH

Ian Rush is the greatest Liverpool goalscorer of all time. He notched up 346 goals in 658 appearances for the Reds.

Born in St Asaph, Flintshire, Ian Rush came to the attention of football scouts when he registered 72 goals in one season as an eleven-year-old schoolboy. In

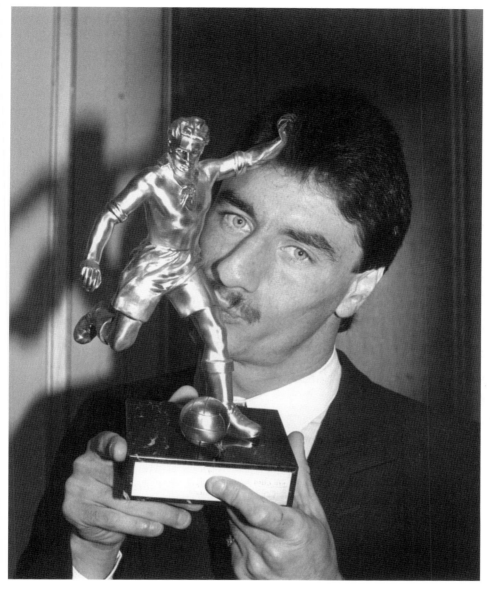

Ian Rush kisses the Footballer of the Year trophy after being voted the 1984 recipient of this prestigious award.

1978 he joined Chester City and under the guidance of Chester manager, Alan Oaks, the lean Welsh teenager began to notch up goals on a regular basis. Every top team in the country decided to run the rule over Chester's goalscoring sensation. Rush hoped that his boyhood heroes, Everton, would take him to

Goodison, but it was Bob Paisley who decided to gamble £300,000 on the teenager. It was a record fee at the time for a teenage footballer.

Chester boss, Alan Oaks, had warned Ian Rush that his early days at Anfield would be hard and he was proved correct. Rush found it hard to settle at Liverpool and was in awe of the star names he was now rubbing shoulders with. Some at Anfield, including Alan Hansen, thought Rush would struggle to make the grade and that an early departure was on the cards. A frustrated Bob Paisley told the painfully shy Rush that he had to assert himself more and become more selfish in front of goal.

In the 1981 Football League Cup final replay against West Ham, Rush was selected by Paisley to replace the injured Steve Heighway. He had made his Liverpool first-team debut three months earlier replacing Kenny Dalglish in a 1-1 draw at Ipswich in December 1980. Ian Rush's Villa Park appearance against West Ham was only his second game for the Reds, but it was the day that the kid from North Wales announced to the world that Liverpool had another star on their hands. He hit the West Ham crossbar in an impressive display for the Reds. Goals from Dalglish and Hansen gave Liverpool a 2-1 victory.

After Ian Rush's first taste of glory with Liverpool in their League Cup triumph over West Ham, he became a first-team regular at Anfield. The goals began to flow on a regular basis after he notched up two against Leeds on his first League appearance of the 1981/82 season. Liverpool ended the season as champions and Ian Rush scored an impressive 17 goals in 32 appearances. Ian Rush also collected another League Cup winners' medal, scoring one of the Liverpool goals in their 3-1 victory over Spurs in the final, Ronnie Whelan scoring the other two. Rush in fact scored an outstanding eight goals in Liverpool's 1981/82 League Cup campaign.

Ian Rush's Liverpool career looked like it had come to an end when he signed for Italian giants Juventus in 1987 for a £3.2 million fee. Rush's Italian experience was not, however, a happy chapter in the Welsh striker's career and a £2.8 million transfer fee brought him back to his spiritual home at Anfield in 1988.

By the time he left Liverpool to join Leeds United in 1996, Ian Rush had accumulated five League Championship, five League Cup, three FA Cup and one European Cup winner's medals during his Anfield career. He was also capped 73 times by Wales and voted Footballer of the Year in 1984.

It is highly unlikely that Liverpool will ever have a goalscoring genius of Ian Rush's calibre again.

Steve Staunton

STEVE STAUNTON

Steve Staunton was born in Drogheda in the Irish Republic. After a spell with the League of Ireland team, Dundalk, Staunton signed for Liverpool in September 1986. The £20,000 fee that Kenny Dalglish paid for Staunton looked the bargain of the century when Dalglish introduced him into the Liverpool side in 1988.

Staunton made his League debut against Spurs on 17 September 1988. The young Irish defender came on as a substitute for Jan Molby in the Reds' 1-1 draw at Anfield. Peter Beardsley scored the Liverpool goal. Steve Staunton made 21 appearances for Liverpool during the 1988/89 campaign and ended up with an FA Cup winners' medal.

With his ability to play in either defence or midfield, Steve Staunton looked to be a formidable acquisition to Dalglish's Liverpool squad. He picked up a League Championship medal in 1990 after Liverpool won the title by nine points from Aston Villa. The 1989/90 season was also notable for Steve Staunton when he managed to score a hat-trick for the Reds against Wigan Athletic in a Football League Cup tie on 4 October 1989. Liverpool won the game 3-0, and 8-2 on aggregate.

In the 1990/91 season Steve Staunton made 24 appearances in the League for Liverpool, but the departure of Kenny Dalglish as manager heralded the end of Staunton's career at Anfield. New boss Graeme Souness decided to sell the twenty-two-year-old full-back to Aston Villa for £1.1 million in July 1991. At this stage in his career Staunton was an established Republic of Ireland international and, with youth on his side, looked to be destined for a long career at Anfield. Souness, however, found Staunton surplus to requirements and Ron Atkinson was delighted to take him to Villa Park. As expected, Steve Staunton developed into one of the most consistent performers in the Premiership and Liverpool's loss was Villa's gain. Staunton had a long and distinguished career at Aston Villa and is currently the manager of Eire.

DAVID BURROWS

Born in Dudley, Worcestershire, David Burrows served his football apprenticeship at West Bromwich Albion and signed professional forms with them in 1986. The strong tackling full-back made only 46 appearances for West Brom before Kenny Dalglish made the Second Division team a £500,000 offer for Burrows in October 1988. The Midlands club accepted and Burrows made his debut against Coventry City on the 22 October 1988. The game ended in a disappointing 0-0 draw. David Burrows made 21 League appearances for the Reds during the 1988/89 season and looked to be a solid acquisition to Dalglish's squad.

The following season saw Burrows playing his part in the Reds' successful title-winning campaign and he appeared 26 times for the new champions of England. With his all-action style and boundless enthusiasm, David Burrows became one of Liverpool's most accomplished performers during Graeme Souness's era as manager at Anfield.

David Burrows

He was a first-team regular during the early 1990s and played his part in Liverpool winning the FA Cup in 1992. There was even talk of full international recognition for the young full-back who had already represented England at Under-21 level. It therefore came as something of a surprise when Graeme Souness decided to tempt West Ham United with an offer of cash, plus David Burrows, in exchange for their own no-nonsense full-back Julian Dicks in September 1993. Not surprisingly West Ham accepted when Souness also threw in Reds' midfielder Mike Marsh, along with Burrows and a hefty cheque.

David Burrows stayed at Upton Park for only a year before to returning to Merseyside when Everton came calling for his services in September 1994. Burrows' Goodison Park adventure lasted less than six months. Coventry City, under the managership of Ron Atkinson, offered Everton most of the £1 million-plus outlay that they had paid to West Ham for Burrows' services and he returned to the Midlands in March 1995.

GARY GILLESPIE

Gary Gillespie signed for Liverpool in July 1983. Joe Fagan needed cover for the outstanding Alan Hansen/Mark Lawrenson combination in central defence for Liverpool, and the tall, commanding Gillespie fitted the bill perfectly. The transfer fee was £325,000 from Coventry City.

Gillespie began his career playing in schools football in his native Stirling and signed for Falkirk in 1977. Coventry signed Gillespie in March 1978 for a £75,000 fee. After 171 games for the Midland club, Gillespie moved to Anfield in 1983.

Gillespie made his full debut against Walsall in a League (Milk) Cup semi-final tie on 7 February 1984. Liverpool drew 2-2, Ronnie Whelan scoring the two goals. Gillespie had to wait until the following season to play in a League game for the Reds, coming on as a substitute in Liverpool's 1-0 defeat at Spurs on the 12 October 1984.

Gary Gillespie

Gary Gillespie played enough games in the 1985/86 campaign to qualify for a League Championship medal. He was also destined to win two more League titles with the Reds in the 1987/88 and 1989/90 seasons. Gillespie's best campaigns for League appearances came during the 1986/87 season when he made 37 appearances and in 1987/88 when he played in 35 League games. Gary Gillespie also represented Scotland 13 times between the years 1987-1990.

In Europe, Gillespie appeared in the ill-fated Heysel final in 1985, coming on as a substitute for Mark Lawrenson when the match against Juventus was barely a minute old.

Gary Gillespie left Anfield for Celtic in August 1991 after 203 appearances for Liverpool. His tally of 16 goals for the Reds, including an impressive hat-trick against Birmingham City in Liverpool's 5-0 victory in April 1986, was quite useful for a central defender. After a three-year spell at Celtic, Gillespie returned to Coventry City on a free transfer in August 1994.

BARRY VENISON

Barry Venison was born in Consett, County Durham. He became an apprentice at Sunderland in the late 1970s and turned professional in 1982. Venison could play in either of the full-back positions; he was also equally adept as a central defender or in a midfield role. At Sunderland Venison developed into quite an accomplished right-back and made 173 appearances for them between 1981 and 1985.

Kenny Dalglish was impressed by Barry Venison's initiative when he wrote to him after Sunderland were struggling in the lower regions of the Second Division in 1986. Venison told Dalglish that he would welcome the opportunity to display his defensive qualities at Anfield. Liverpool offered Sunderland £250,000 for Venison and the full-back's cheeky approach to the Reds' boss had come up trumps.

Barry Venison made his League debut against Newcastle United on the opening day of the 1986/87 season. Two goals from Ian Rush gave the Reds a 2-0 victory in the 23 August 1986 fixture. Venison made 33 appearances during Liverpool's 1986/87 campaign, playing in both full-back positions. The following season saw Venison pick up a League Championship medal after playing in 18 of Liverpool's fixtures. FA Cup success in the 1988/89 campaign meant that Venison had won the English game's two main prizes in just three seasons at Anfield. Liverpool won the League title again in 1990 and Barry Venison appeared in 25 of the Reds' fixtures.

Barry Venison

Injuries then restricted Barry Venison's Liverpool appearances over the following two seasons and with his first-team chances at Anfield looking scarce, he signed for Newcastle in July 1992 for £250,000. Venison had made 151 appearances for Liverpool during his stint at Anfield.

Barry Venison proved himself to be a highly efficient performer at Newcastle and his full-back displays brought international recognition in 1994. Venison made his England debut against the USA at Wembley in September 1994. Alan Shearer scored England's goals in a 2-0 victory. Venison was awarded one more England cap against Uruguay in March 1995.

Barry Venison ended his career with a season playing for Galatasaray and then back in England at Southampton.

Bibliography

BOOKS

Aldridge, J., with Jawad, H., *John Aldridge: My Story* (Hodder & Stoughton, 1999)

Anderson, J., with Done, S., *The Official Liverpool FC Illustrated History* (Carlton, 2002)

Barrett, N., *The Daily Telegraph Football Chronicle* (Ebury Press (Carlton), 1996)

Grobbelaar, B., *More Than Somewhat* (Collins Willow, 1986)

Houghton, R., *Ray Houghton's Liverpool Notebook: Inside Anfield 1988-89*

Johnston, C., with Jameson, N., *The Craig Johnston Story* (Fleetwood Books, 1990)

Liversedge, S., *Liverpool The Official Centenary History* (Hamlyn, 1991)

Molby, J., with Lloyd, G., *Jan the Man: From Anfield to Vetch Field* (Victor Gollancz, 1999)

Nawrat, C. and Hutchings, S., *The Sunday Times Illustrated History of Football* (Ted Smart, 1995)

Phillips, D., *Better Than The Brazilians: Liverpool FC's 1987-88 Season* (Carnegie Publishing, 1999)

Rush, I., *Rush* (Arthur Barker Ltd, 1985)

Signy, D. and Giller, N., *Golden Heroes: Fifty Seasons of Footballer of the Year* (Chameleon Books, 1997)

Watt, T., and Palmer, K., *Wembley: The Greatest Stage* (Simon & Schuster, 1998)

OTHER PUBLICATIONS

Four Four Two Magazine
The Daily Express

The Daily Star
The Daily Telegraph
The Guardian
The Liverpool Daily Post
The Liverpool Echo
The Liverpool Football Echo
The Liverpool Matchday Programme
The Kop Magazine
The Mirror
The Sunday Mirror
The Times

OTHER SOURCES

Bob Paisley's Personal View of The Liverpool First Team Squad of 1986–87
BBC Radio 5 Live
BBC Radio Merseyside

SPECIAL THANKS

Holly Bennion, Rob Sharman and all at Tempus Publishing
Graham, Louise, Linda and Helen.

Other titles published by Stadia

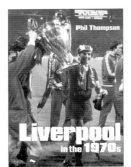

Liverpool in the 1970s
PHIL THOMPSON

When the legendary Liverpool manager Bill Shankly retired in 1974 he was leaving in place at Anfield the second outstanding team that he had assembled. With new boss Bob Paisley at the helm, trophy after trophy found its way to Anfield, the team achieving immortality with European Cup wins in 1977 and 1978, and by the end of the decade the Reds were firmly established as one of the great clubs in world football. This book documents, in words and pictures, the sensational exploits of Liverpool in the 1970s.

0 7524 3431 4

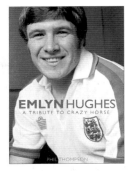

Emlyn Hughes A Tribute to Crazy Horse
PHIL THOMPSON

Whether it was as a flamboyant footballer whose distinctive style earned him the nickname 'Crazy Horse', or as the *Question of Sport* captain who rubbed shoulders with royalty, Emlyn Hughes never did things by half. Making his name at Liverpool FC, he helped the club to four League titles, an FA Cup victory and two UEFA Cup titles. Between 1967 and 1979 he made 665 appearances for the Reds during which time he led them to their first two European Cups in 1977 and 1978.

0 7524 3953 7

The England Managers The Impossible Job
BRIAN SCOVELL

Since 1946 when Walter Winterbottom became the first England manager, the position has always attracted frenzied and critical headlines. Ramsey and Robson, arguably the most successful, weren't wanted, Don Revie deserted to Dubai, Graham Taylor had to go and Eriksson's departure was dramatically announced in the lead-up to the 2006 World Cup Finals. This look back at the men in 'the impossible job' is laced with insights and behind-the-scenes anecdotes, making it a compelling read for all football fans.

0 7524 3748 8

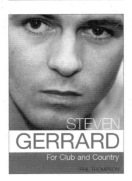

Steven Gerrard For Club and Country
PHIL THOMPSON

Skilful and aggressive, Steven Gerrard has a knack of scoring spectacular goals for club and country. Now captain of Liverpool FC, Gerrard has already led his side to Champions League glory and, having signed a new four-year contract in the summer of 2005, supporters hope his drive and dynamism will lead them on to many more successes in the future. Including a comprehensive collection of illustrations, this is the compelling story of a nation's hero.

0 7524 3793 3

If you are interested in purchasing other books published by Stadia, or in case you have difficulty finding any Stadia books in your local bookshop, you can also place orders directly through the Tempus Publishing website
www.tempus-publishing.com